Accelerating Unity Through Automation

Power Up Your Unity Workflow by Offloading Intensive Tasks

Simon Jackson

Apress®

Accelerating Unity Through Automation: Power Up Your Unity Workflow by Offloading Intensive Tasks

Simon Jackson
Warrington, Cheshire, UK

ISBN-13 (pbk): 978-1-4842-9507-6
https://doi.org/10.1007/978-1-4842-9508-3

ISBN-13 (electronic): 978-1-4842-9508-3

Managing Director, Apress Media LLC: Welmoed Spahr
Acquisitions Editor: Spandana Chatterjee
Development Editor: Spandana Chatterjee
Editorial Assistant: Mark Powers

Cover designed by eStudioCalamar

Cover image Boliva Inteligente on Unsplash (www.unsplash.com)

Distributed to the book trade worldwide by Springer Science+Business Media New York, 1 New York Plaza, Suite 4600, New York, NY 10004-1562, USA. Phone 1-800-SPRINGER, fax (201) 348-4505, e-mail orders-ny @springer-sbm.com, or visit www.springeronline.com. Apress Media, LLC is a California LLC and the sole member (owner) is Springer Science + Business Media Finance Inc (SSBM Finance Inc). SSBM Finance Inc is a **Delaware** corporation.

For information on translations, please e-mail booktranslations@springernature.com; for reprint, paperback, or audio rights, please e-mail bookpermissions@springernature.com.

Apress titles may be purchased in bulk for academic, corporate, or promotional use. eBook versions and licenses are also available for most titles. For more information, reference our Print and eBook Bulk Sales web page at http://www.apress.com/bulk-sales.

Any source code or other supplementary material referenced by the author in this book is available to readers on GitHub (github.com/Apress). For more detailed information, please visit https://www.apress.com/gp/services/source-code.

Paper in this product is recyclable

Table of Contents

About the Author

Simon Jackson is a proud educator, showing developers how to make the most of modern technology to enable them to build the best they can using the tools of today and tomorrow. He is a father/husband and engineer who is always breaking down new tech and learning something every day in order to expand his horizons as well, as having as much fun as possible along the way. Alongside his work in XR working with the best and brightest to build the next generation of tech, he is also a strong supporter of open source and publishing tools and features to accelerate every developer's workflow.

About the Technical Reviewer

 **Jesús Ángel Pérez-Roca Fernández** is a professor from A Coruña, Spain. He teaches web programming using HTML, CSS, JavaScript, and React. He also teaches mobile development using Java and Kotlin and video game development using Unity and C#. He loves programming and learning new skills, so he enrolls in several online courses and watches YouTube tutorials about new technologies, frameworks, and programming skills. He is also an active member of local technological communities where they gather to talk about Python, Java, web technologies, and many other subjects while drinking a few beers. In his free time, he likes going to the cinema to watch movies, but what he loves most is binge-watching series sitting on the sofa.

CHAPTER 1

What Is Automation?

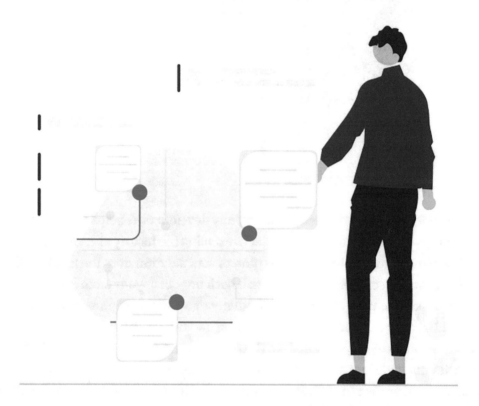

Welcome to this title which aims to save you both time and money with just a small investment of your most precious commodity for any Unity developer, neurons (brain matter :D), and thanks to this title, far less than would be expended by going at it alone or, worse, asking for help on your social feeds.

Automation, often seen as a dark art or long-lost treasure that is hard to seek and even harder to find, can save you countless hours of repetitive tasks and look ahead to help avoid troubles on the road before you plummet off the cliff of despair, such as when Apple suddenly does not accept builds with feature X, because Unity…

© Simon Jackson 2023
S. Jackson, *Accelerating Unity Through Automation*, https://doi.org/10.1007/978-1-4842-9508-3_1

What Does Automation Mean for a Unity Developer?

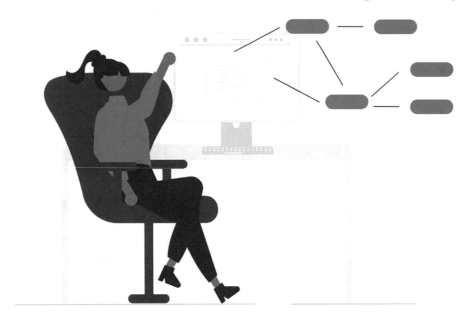

Source control has long been used by most Unity developers; it helps to protect the investments you make in your Unity project, revealing the history of your code, and provides you an almost foolproof way to protect your solution from the impacts of upgrading your project. Whether it is a small hack project or your main income, source control gives us a measure of protection from the rigors of development, especially when our beloved development machine decides to spend time with the fairies (provided you check in and push before you shut down last night, you did push last night, didn't you?).

But with our code and project hosted on source control, many do not see the advantages of, or are aware of, the power that comes from our code being online, even in a private repository. Having code available online means it can be analyzed, checked, validated, and even built for us, all without lifting a finger. If you are also part of a larger team, it gives opportunities to reduce workloads on teams "checking" code to ensure it meets a standard before giving a senior dev the nod to look it over, saving countless hours of shaking heads and fists. I have lost count of the many times I've pushed a Pull Request (PR) back to a junior developer, simply because they did not format or document their code to the company's standards, time I could have used to get another coffee, a true crime.

We will go into more detail in the next chapter, but as a highlight, here are some of the repetitive tasks that automation can deliver, from the small to very, very large:

- Checking that developers have spelt things correctly

- Validating coding standards to a specification

- Running unit tests automatically to ensure there are no regression issues

- Ensuring code has the appropriate documentation

- For public repos, checking if the contributor is a valid user and is not a bot

- Checking the project builds for all target platforms

- Creating builds and signing packages using secrets

And soooo much more. In one case, I created a pipeline that would automatically up-version the project for each PR that was merged, and when this was published, it would also increase the development version to ensure it was always ahead of what was published.

In some more advanced scenarios, I've seen some pipelines now employing AI to scan code for "known vulnerabilities"; in fact, GitHub now offers this as a generic built-in service, should you wish to enable it. Scanning code on each check-in/push against a wealth of known vulnerable code, such as SQL injection, trojans, and suspicious code that might be rejected by vendor partners or, worse, open your loving title to attack/exploitation.

What to Expect from This Title?

With a grasp of the subject, this title will walk you through the A–Y of automation (z is reserved for future use) as it pertains to building Unity projects. I say Unity projects as this is valid for any Unity project, not just games (I use it even more for my Enterprise solutions). You will get to know the terminology involved and the services available and, given your choice of service, an excellent footing to getting your own automation setup in hours rather than days/weeks.

If implemented correctly, you should almost immediately notice the cost-savings from utilizing automation, and it will eventually lead you to building/adding your own automation techniques that are specific to your requirements; no one path exists for automation as everyone's needs are unique, but they all have common traits.

So, sit back, pull up a fresh brew, adorn your reading glasses if you have them, and let us get started on this journey.

Looking Ahead

Here is a rundown of what to expect:

- What Is Gained Through Automation, the Highlights!
  A walk-through of some of the most common automation tasks and their benefits.

- Services Covered by This Title
  An overview of the common automation platforms available for Unity builders today.

- The Structure of Automation
  A walk-through of the language and terminology of automation.

- Automation Hosting
  If you Should you use online hardware for running your automation, or use your own hardware instead to save some cash, as well as some tips and tricks.

- Validation, Checking Your Code
  A discussion on the many options to validate code, comments, and documentation for your project to ensure it is maintainable and does not incur security risks.

- Testing, Making Sure It Runs
  Should you test or not and the many benefits of ensuring your project is always in a runnable state for all your target platforms.

- Building and Publishing
  Build it and ship it, streamlining the publication process of your dream.

- Setting Up Unity Gaming Services Automation
  An in-depth walk-through into setting up and using Unity's own automation services for managing your project.

- Setting Up Azure DevOps

An in-depth walk-through into setting up and using Microsoft Azure's free automation services for managing your project.

- Setting Up GitHub Actions

   An in-depth walk-through into setting up and using GitHub's free automation services for managing your project.

- Final Notes

   A personal walk-through of the recommended paths for using automation in production projects and some final tips.

I hope you enjoy the journey.

## CHAPTER 2

What Is Gained Through Automation, the Highlights!

The list of possibilities in automation is almost endless, just about anything you would want to happen is available; the only real question is if someone has gone to the effort of publishing a plugin or extension that you can simply call (with parameters) to do the task. And the community does love to publish.

The main challenge when building your automation pipelines is to know how much time to invest in finding pre-built solutions or whether you just build it yourself (and then decide to publish it? maybe).

© Simon Jackson 2023
S. Jackson, *Accelerating Unity Through Automation*, https://doi.org/10.1007/978-1-4842-9508-3_2

To get you started, this chapter will meander through some of the possibilities for the art of the possible to set you on your path, as knowing just what you can do is half the battle, beyond doing just the simple/obvious. Ultimately though, the choice is yours and there is no hard and fast rule for what you should or should not automate, but rather what is right for your organization or even the project. In some instances, I have defined different paths based on the style of the project and who is involved:

- Is the project visible to the public for them to comment/contribute to or is it a private project only used by internal staff?

- How much information do I need to share between projects?

- How critical is the visibility for the velocity/burn-down for a specific project?

- Who needs access to the results/builds, or do certain staff just need notifying?

In some large-scale deployments, functionality and assets are managed independently, and it is only when they are built that they are all pulled together to produce the final version (something used often in large or AAA-style game projects). But with this separation, there are checks and balances needed to ensure managers are kept up to date, and cross-checks are needed to ensure no distance is created between all the separate units.

In smaller projects, just a build will suffice, and in a lot of cases, not even the final build, but just to check it **can** build for **ALL** the target platforms (the sheer amount of times I have been focused on one platform, only to find later an approach is not valid because it does not work on another).

What you do and when you do it is almost as critical as what you do in your automation, but, ultimately, it needs to service **YOUR** needs and requirements and not just be there because someone thought it would be a good idea. Time is money and even more so when you are moving that time to automation, just because a person is not running it, a person still must build and maintain the automation, including all the hardware that is running it incurs a cost somewhere, left unchecked, you could be burning hours and money rather than making savings, just a thought.

Example Workflows

Here are some of the most common tasks that can be achieved through automation to give you a sense of the possible beyond the basics.

1. Checkout

One of the simplest tasks is to check out code from the repository; some automations do this automatically, while others require a specific step to ensure the correct code is pulled. In some cases, this is not the first step, as prechecks can occur to avoid unnecessary bandwidth use, as well as the time it takes to download large repositories.

You must remember, with automation it is unknown if the host that is running the automation has ever seen your code, so do not assume it has cloned the code before. Each run of automation **MUST** be treated as if it is a brand-new machine that must be configured to run your automation; never make assumptions about how the machine is set up!

As indicated earlier, some workflows might require several checkouts to get content stored in various places; if submodules are involved, make sure to set the parameters for the checkout to include submodules as well (do not assume it automatically will). If you have access to the host, you can build up the checkout stage incrementally and just check the working folder the automation is using to see what is downloaded and where to ensure it meets your automation/build specifications.

In one workflow, I built a Unity build pipeline for building and validating a Unity Package (UPM); a UPM package **DOES NOT** have its own Unity project by default, so the automation had to clone the project, generate a NEW Unity project, and then copy the cloned code into the "Packages" folder before any tests or builds could happen.

Getting the code is always the critical step for doing anything, but it may not be your FIRST step if you need to validate that the person that is kicking off the build has the authority to do so (you can also add prechecks to workflows for an admin to approve the workflow to continue) and that they have completed all required tasks before the process continues.

2. Running Scripts – Bash/PowerShell/Python

The most underrated task that any automation can do is to run scripts to do just about anything on the build environment; this can range from simply checking that the required software is installed or that the build host is set up correctly to running command-line tasks to do just about anything. A lot of community-built tasks will include a fair amount of scripting, so it is key that you always have a peek inside those packages to ensure your build host can run those scripts, for example, have Bash or PowerShell installed on your build environment.

If you are using scripts in automation, it is also critical to **SPECIFY** what language or runtime a script is written in for running on the host; this helps both tell the automation what to expect and informs anyone else having to read or update your workflow what it was written for. **NEVER** leave it up to the default as this is different for different types of hosts.

At the end of the day, all automation does eventually resolve down to a command that needs to be executed on the host, which is almost always using a command library native to the host. But remember! Depending on the output of your automation, it may have different host requirements, so the language used SHOULD be balanced to run on them all to save you uncertain headaches in the future.

3. NPM Build and Test

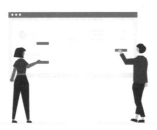

NPM (Node Package Manager) is a favored way of building a lot of projects these days (less so Unity), especially web or service-based projects. It provides an extensive library of functionality to both build and host solutions.

Remember, NPM is built on top of NodeJS which also has other requirements. Make sure either your host or your pipeline includes the critical steps to install both NPM and its dependencies. As stated earlier, you can never assume that the host running your automation has ANY of these dependencies installed, so always check.

As far as automation goes, testing NPM is VERY easy as you can run most of the commands manually on your own machine instead of being wholly dependent on testing through automation; only the paths involved are likely to change; for everything else, you can test to your heart's desires, especially when you are checking the package contains everything you need BEFORE pushing it out to an NPM hosting service like NPMJS.

Building NPM packages from the ground up is always stressful, especially if you are including hidden folders or ensuring you are EXCLUDING critical files that should never make the package. The last thing you want to find in your published package is any secure or sensitive information, as once it is on the "Internet," it is VERY hard to take back. When building packages for publication, test, test, test, both locally and through iteration when building your workflow and checking your package result is what you NEED it to be. I've lost count of the times messing with "npmIgnore" definitions to ensure nothing snuck into the package I did not want.

---

4. MSBuild Build and Test

Like NPM, MSBuild and "dotnet" are some favored ways to produce and build solutions or packages; with .NET6, this has gotten even more common with the ability to produce single executables for projects. Even with Unity projects, additional tasks are usually needed to run MSBuild or Xcode on the output of a Unity Build to eventually get a solution that a client can run; these are, at times, the most stressful parts of constructing a working workflow due to the intricate (and often undocumented) command parameters needed to get the compiler to produce what you need (which is usually just a few clicks doing it manually in the code editor).

When looking for MSBuild/Xcode parameters, use SEVERAL sources for comparison and never trust a single article to tell you how to get it working. You might get lucky, but in my experience, a quick comparison is your friend so you can understand what each parameter is doing and which are the critical parameters to get your project published.

---

5. Chat/Mail Integration (Slack/Email)

Sometimes, people just want to know something happened, something good, something bad, or just that the coffee machine is ready for that next brew of its sweet sultry sauce. There are many custom plugins out there to do all the hard work for you, and you get to control what the message is and when it is published; sometimes, these are done as webhooks from your chat software (both Discord and Slack support webhooks for talking/listening to APIs), but relying on the API is troublesome as there is little to no control.

By building notifications into your workflows, you can control the message, ensuring that only interested parties are notified and when. This is often overlooked, but I have found it invaluable in ensuring the right channels for communication for the most repetitive questions. Stop asking me when the build has finished, check this slack channel! (Or even build a slack bot that can query the automation API that someone can fire a command at to query it.)

6. Schedule/Remove Backups

Not all projects are just code, or even code and assets, some also include backend databases or APIs that need to be consumed. Critically, these also need to be tested before the next build is pushed out to production and "hopefully" not destroying half the backend in the process. So, these also need to be included in automation while testing, but no one should ever test on a live system (should they?), and automation helps here, scripting a backup of the live service to use or restoring the most recent backup and spinning up the environment to test against, a real life/time-saver.

Also, when the eventual push to production comes, automation can force a backup BEFORE the critical task begins to further mitigate any risks during the upgrade and giving you an almost instantaneous restore if indeed the publication fails, as well as the critical "oh darn" workflow to automatically restore the production site from the most recent (or targeted) restore point. If left to manual hands, it always costs more in time and money with the eventual risks of "human error," so having done this from the point of publication goes a long way to reducing those risks and frees up the time for the technical team who manages it.

7. Upload Artifacts, Build, and Publish

If everything is successful, the dates have been met and everyone who needs to be informed has been informed, it is great when automation can simply flick a switch and push out your latest and greatest (or as in the previous example, go back VERY, VERY QUICKLY). This publication might be just to the source site, such as GitHub, or even package/solution hosting sites like OpenUPM or NPMJS; wherever your package needs to be, there is usually an API or service where you can push it to.

In many projects I have managed, especially when you are flitting between a full release and development "preview" packages, it is always comforting that I do not need to do anything, it just all happens automagically through automation. Once a PR has been merged with development, out pops a new preview release that consumers can pick up if they want to.

---

8. Create Releases on GitHub

Like with publishing, source sites like GitHub and others provide APIs to enable you to create releases directly on their site, allowing consumers to always see the latest release when browsing or get notifications because they subscribed to hear about them. There are also tags (a pointer to a specific check-in) that can be monitored and, in the case of OpenUPM, used to create a release for you on their platform.

9. Update Project Management Solutions and Workflows

Fed up with your project manager walking up to your desk or emailing you for a status update, then get automation to automatically update their project plan directly for all their critical facts and figures. It will not stop them from pestering, but it should reduce the chatter that always gets in the way of coding (and everyone knows that getting interrupted always costs you time to get back into the flow).

There are many integrations available in the community, most provided by the vendors of those solutions, and failing that, there is usually an API you can utilize. One of the most creative solutions I have seen involved using scripting to effectively do UI testing and force-clicked/updated the actual software, certainly not for the faint of heart, but that dev was never asked for an update again, such bliss.

10. Generate Release Documentation

One of the most tedious tasks in any release is always collating the release notes for what has changed since the last push. Thankfully, the rest of the community agrees with you, and there are MANY extensions available to use to build, create, and format release notes to your preference. Granted, this also means you MUST ensure that both yourself and your team write PROPER commit messages (you DO WRITE GOOD COMMIT MESSAGES?) and/or use a form for populating PRs.

But this is truly a lifesaver for a lot of projects. If you want to vet the release note, then you can always include an "approve" step in your workflow to check the content before it ships; you know, JUST IN CASE! :D

11. Publish Documentation

Like release notes, you can also use the likes of DOCFX to generate your documentation for you and publish to your docs site or even GitHub pages, granted this is provided you have ensured you have added the correct documentation tags to your code (and not done a "Unity" of late, such a shame their docs used to be soooo good). You can include automated checks to ensure the Summary and Include tags have been filled in on PR submission (or on push in some cases), which increases the value of the documentation.

Personally, I have started to mandate that code be documented, even in hack projects. If you cannot learn from the project and later understand why something was done the way it is, then you can never truly learn, and future you (or replacements) will never understand. Yes, it can be a pain but saves you in the long run; in fact, sometimes while documenting a method, it has forced me to question whether it is even needed or if something could be better!

In some cases, I have seen documentation building as an additional type of test, because if the docs cannot compile but the code can, then it can indicate referencing issues in your final solution that your unit tests might be missing/lacking.

12. Varying Flows Based on the Submitter

There is no rule that every test needs to be run, and in circumstances where additional checks are not required, you might run a full battery of tests for junior programmers and skip some for seniors (although personally, I test everything, every time!). But you might also want to change the reporting based on who submitted the Pull Request (or even who commented), so it is very useful that most automation provides you with an almost unlimited number of variations to quantify what runs when.

It is worth investing some time to see what API endpoints and conditions the likes of GitHub provide (most source sites have the same) to extend your workflow to add additional steps for certain conditions or even skip steps for certain groups/individuals.

But do not go overboard and remember the KISS principle; only add variation where it adds value or can save processing time where you know you do not need to spend it!

---

13. Call External APIs for Analytics, Reporting, or PowerBI

Integration is critical in most workflows, especially when you are operating in a large environment. Yes, the UI does give you certain details, but it can sometimes be awkward to get stats from. Most workflow systems have an extensive ability to integrate with third-party APIs (as indicated earlier) and should not be overlooked for externalizing the performance details of your workflows.

It also goes a long way with "management" if they have great charts and pretty things they can point to with all the investment in automation, which PowerBI is outstanding for and worth a look at.

14. Generate/Search for Gifs to Add to a Post/Issue When Craziness Is Detected or a "lmgtfy" Tag Is Used by an Admin

Not all automations have to be serious; quite regularly (if I can get away with it) on public projects, I will add some simple but effective workflows to save me time replying to snarky or badly written questions that could have been resolved simply by putting the title of a query into a search engine rather than wasting my time having to read an issue posted.

So having comment triggers that look for predefined text (like lmgtfy – let me get/ Google that for you) and post a random gif in its place helps to liven up any tedious discourse.

I may or may not have in the past also had some workflows to translate some queries to Klingon, just for fun… Who knows what could be done with some integration to ChatGPT too these days, just saying….

---

15. Convert Source Files (yaml/xml/json) to Other Formats or Perform Bespoke Actions

There are some things for which automation is VERY well suited, especially when it comes to tedious tasks. I have regularly moved some build tasks back into the automation and used configuration files to perform the required tasks; this has ranged from

- Generating tile/map sets for games

- Doing first-pass translation files for sending to a translation party to review (with caching of course)

- Defining color swatches/sets for use in terrain painting

- Building character models from randomly generated body parts for review

Essentially, if you can derive configuration for a complex task, you can have automation generate that content for you, especially useful if sometimes that generation is complex, and you don't want to lose access to your machine while it runs.

16. Integrate with Docker/Kubernetes

Not all automation runs on a physical host, just as not all solutions are deployed to physical hosts. Containers are evolving deployments more and more these days, and automation can help significantly with the management and testing of these containers before they see the light of day.

These are generally integrated as "services" that most automation pipelines can recognize, with container registries being built into the backend of most automation platforms, especially as most automation also happens on virtual hosts for the most basic tasks. It usually requires dedicated paid use to have physical hardware in the cloud these days.

This availability even extends to Database systems, as shown by the GitHub Services Examples, showing integrations with MongoDB, Postgres, and Redis.

17. Manage Versioning

One of the first things I stand up in any workflow, especially when I need to release packages to the open source world, is versioning. Never having to worry if I have incremented a version number between patch, minor, and major releases is a huge relief.

Just make sure you capture all the points where versioning is critical. Unity is especially annoying by having multiple places where the version of the built application is recorded (BundleVersion, MetroVersion, ...Version); they are easy enough to handle with some quick regex (simple, lol), you just need to be aware.

18. Run Unit Tests and Perform Actions Based on Results

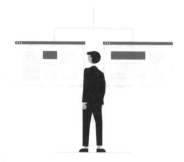

Testing, if done correctly, can be a lifesaver. Granted, it is neither the easiest nor time-friendly task, and most developers will shun it for an easier life; however, without testing you are leaving the health of your project to chance or experience, but remembering that not everyone has the same experience and, additionally, also has "their own way of doing things."

The larger the project, the more critical it is to have dedicated unit testing in place, although personally, if something is crucial enough, however small, I generally will add tests to ensure it always operates at least the way I want it and given time, but also to check that it does not fall flat on its face when the unexpected happens. I have lost count of the times I have been stuck in an endless loop of figuring out why Unity is crashing, only to find it was due to it injecting a NULL because the scene was loading (did you know that Unity loads scenes TWICE when starting in play mode, once to initialize the scene, then it unloads, and then it runs? If you have code that is "run" dependently, it is VERY annoying).

My advice is to ALWAYS add tests, and if you are not used to writing tests, then at least learn the basics, and then have automation check those tests on each check-in and/or build to save your skin for when the unthinkable happens. There are also those who write tests to build code (Test-Driven Development; however, I am not one of those developers), and there is value in having decent test coverage for your app/game.

References

To sum up the wonder that is this chapter, here are some of the sources used to compile this list; it is in no way extensive as there are SOOO many possibilities when it comes to automation, from the mission critical to the dastardly hilarious (I have seen pipelines that check if you have 2FA enabled on your account and will spam you if you do not!).

Have fun with the further reading:

- The awesome list of awesome GitHub Actions

  `https://github.com/sdras/awesome-actions`

- Google's list of its own GitHub Actions

  `https://github.com/actions`

- The official Azure Marketplace for DevOps extensions

  `https://marketplace.visualstudio.com/azuredevops/`

- Check out Dino's awesome Unity build tasks

  `www.unitydevops.com/`

There are many resources out there, some you will use right away, others you can use for inspiration for building your own private automations; there is no wrong way really, learn from the best, but just be sure to give credit where credit is due if you start publishing your own.

Summary

In this chapter, we have covered the majority of the critical tasks that automation can be used for to speed up our lives and save us time on the most repetitive of tasks.

What is covered here is not exhaustive as the "art of the possible" is almost boundless when it comes to automation; if you can think, write, or dream it on your local machine, then the same is possible through automation. In some cases, I have "gone beyond" and even wrote utilities through automation (a script to validate images for their use as AR tracking targets using the Google tools, for example).

Dream big and let us get on with the main show.

CHAPTER 3

Services Covered by This Title

Through this title, we will cover the three main contenders for automating the build of your Unity project, although there are many others out there with varying levels of cost and functionality; in this chapter, we will review these contenders and give you the kinds of information you need to use when validating the various alternative possibilities out there such as Bitbucket, GitLab, and others.

If there are any terms covered in this chapter you are not familiar with, check out Chapter 4 which covers terminology and more.

© Simon Jackson 2023
S. Jackson, *Accelerating Unity Through Automation*, https://doi.org/10.1007/978-1-4842-9508-3_3

Cost

One of the keenest deciding factors in choosing an automation provider is cost, which can come in many forms, such as

- Runtime costs – Ongoing operation costs for running your automation services.

- Hardware costs – If you are running your own servers.

- Maintenance costs – This includes the time taken for someone or a team to initially set up the automation and to maintain it over time.

There is always a cost involved in implementing automation, whether it is time spent or vendor charges when builds are running; however, the benefits will almost always outweigh the costs (depending on how much you are paying) by reducing the time taken to perform repetitive tasks (making builds and distributing them is a real burden for ongoing management) and identifying issues earlier in the development cycle, and at all critical junctions (build, test, packaging, and delivery), any issue identified BEFORE the customer gets their hand on your project can save both your reputation and in the worse cases money.

Ultimately, it comes down to how much you are spending to get your final product into the hands of your users and the time involved vs. a small investment to ensure this is safe, secure, and valid. For smaller teams or individuals, this can be a larger investment but is a real time-saver later. For larger teams, it is even more critical due to how much is invested in making the product in the first place, and everything that can be done to ensure the output is safe should be done to protect that investment.

Use Cases

I have personally used all the services listed here over many years, as they have grown, developed, been enhanced, and in some cases replaced; they all have their benefits and detriments (which I will highlight), but in the majority of late as things have improved, I have learned more to open vendor solutions that let me build what I need and customize it how I like as my skills have improved over packages and black box solutions which provide convenience over complexity.

The Reality Collective

The Reality Collective, much like its predecessor the XRTK, has quite an extensive collection of components called UPM packages (Unity Package Manager) that can be consumed by a Unity project; thus, it does not have a "Unity Project" to speak of (except for a developer hub project that tests them collectively). This proved quite a challenge in automation to begin testing and building; it required the creation of a temporary Unity project (which Unity does not make easy) to run the required Unity builds and tests to validate the package.

If you need to build Unity assets/packages, I encourage you to have a walk through the extensive GitHub Actions workflows (once you understand them) if you have similar requirements. There are many packages involved in the project with varying requirements and dependencies which need to be managed to build and test the entire framework.

The Unity UI Extensions Project

This project required similar requirements to the Reality Collective but on a much smaller scale (being a single package). Originally, it ran its automation on Bitbucket but recently moved to GitHub as the Bitbucket native automation had some limitations which did not suit the project. The capabilities between the two providers are quite similar, but I have found of late that Microsoft's migration of critical behaviors from Azure to GitHub Actions has really powered up GitHub's offering.

Several Business Clients

In working with many enterprise clients, the needs for building automation have varied drastically depending on their requirements. Many have opted for Unity Cloud Build for simplicity, just needing to create builds quickly and opting for the Higher Subscriptions (Pro ➤ Enterprise) to gain benefits in operation costs. For many others, I have used a split method of using GitHub Actions to provide frontline support for their codebase and inspection and then using Azure Pipelines for build and shipping.

Ultimately, the path you take must be right for your project.

Open Source

When doing game jams and other prototype projects, I have almost always leaned on automation using pre-built templates and community-driven resources to get simple and quick automation up and running early; this saves countless hours of broken builds and wrong turns, even for the smallest of projects. Granted NOT all, quick technical projects are almost never automated, but ultimately, I always turn to an automation service to save myself.

You do not want to find out weeks or months later that either you or a compatriot has accidentally checked in license or API keys into your repository. Once that is in there, it's hard to get out without a great deal of pain, or worse, as everything that is on the Internet is always findable by someone.

On to the Services

With the preamble out of the way, let us dig into the services this book will cover, namely:

- Unity Gaming Services – DevOps
- Azure Pipelines
- GitHub Actions

With each provider, we will review the costs involved and a comparison of the features each provides, including

- Source Control Integration – What popular source control providers does the vendor integrate with?
- Self-Hosting – Can you use your own hardware to run the automation or not?
- Custom Pipelines – How much can you customize the build process?
- Unity Project Building – Unity project building considerations.
- Build Distribution – How easy is it to distribute builds for testing?
- Packaging – Does the solution offer packaging/hosting support?
- Deployment – Can you automate the delivery of the project to stores?
- Analytics – Does the provider have any analytic offerings and are they integrated?
- Other Integrations – Are there any other useful integrations offered by the provider?

Unity Gaming Services – DevOps

Since Unity 5, Unity has provided an automated build solution to address the need to offload time-critical activities to backend operations, constantly evolving the service to address the needs of its community. However, this is provided as an "off-the-shelf" solution that can only be operated by Unity itself and seen as a revenue offering for Unity.

Not to say that is bad, as Unity is wholly responsible for the operation of its DevOps environment which a fair few partners prefer, to ensure that their projects are maintained and managed by Unity's dedicated team, although this does come at a cost of flexibility due to the streamlined nature of its environment.

There is flexibility in places, but it becomes harder to implement anything other than what Unity itself provides. That being said, there is a community of developers who do provide some extensions (such as publishing to Steam), but these are not directly supported by Unity as they are extensions to their in-house service.

Costs Involved

There are no packaged options for Unity Cloud Build, and it is only offered on a per-use (pay as you go) plan; essentially, you pay for what you use (Figure 3-1).

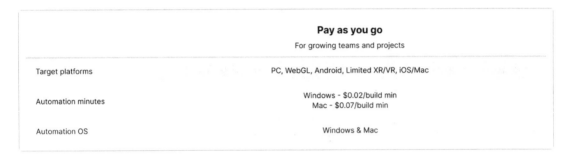

Figure 3-1. *Unity Cloud Build pricing*

It is worth noting that Unity admits in its FAQ that build times in Cloud Build can be longer than a standalone build: "Builds with Cloud Build can be 2–3 times as long as a local build, but this also depends on the size of your project. Beware shader compilation times!"

There is a local hosting option, but it is NOT using the Unity Cloud System, but, instead, Unity provides a "Unity Build Server" option for which you get one license with Unity Pro, and if you want more, then you might need to build additional licenses or upgrade to Unity Enterprise licensing.

Comparison

Table 3-1 shows a comparison of the standard features in automation as it pertains to Unity DevOps.

Table 3-1. *Comparing standard automation features pertaining to Unity DevOps*

Feature	Level of Support	Simplicity	Critical Notes
Source Control Integration	Plastic SCM (Unity), Git (GitHub/Bitbucket/ GitLab), Apache Subversion, Perforce	Out-of-the-box integration, guided	Your source control project may need a specific configuration to run in Unity Cloud Build, especially if you use submodules
Self-Hosting	Not for Cloud Build	N/A	Separate Unity Build system with Unity Pro available
Custom Pipelines	Not directly	Complex	Build process is extendable through pre-/post-build scripts in the Unity project using #if UNITY_CLOUD_BUILD compiler definition to protect local builds (see ScriptHooks, under built targets)
Unity Project Building	Yes	Mostly easy	Some complexity when things go wrong
Build Distribution	Yes, with email support built in	Built-in	Other distributions are manual through integrations
Packaging	Local Build packaging	Easy	
Deployment	Limited	Fairly easy	Android only, mainly for handling multiple Android Stores
Analytics	Available as a plugin service for app/build monitoring	Fairly easy	
Other Integrations	Unity offers webhooks, Discord, Slack, Email, Jira, Trello	Good clear documentation, built-in	For the direct services, the UI for setting them up is very clear, webhooks can be tricky

Personal Comments

Overall, if you just want a quick solution to get a Unity project built, Unity Cloud Build is fairly quick and easy to use, and you can get it running in about an hour. But you are charged for every build whether it works or not, even if the build fault is Unity. There are no plans for Plus, Pro, or Enterprise users, everyone pays the same regardless (although Pro and Enterprise do have the separate option of a Unity Build Server).

When it comes to publishing to a store, you are on your own (except for Android), even the Apple Store (which surprises me, I could have sworn it was supported in the past). You can work around this with ScriptHooks and have builds call external services/deployments to fill the gap, but you are on your own if it fails.

Azure Pipelines

Microsoft's DevOps offering (Azure Pipelines) has been the long stay of managing large enterprise projects, ensuring that huge investments were secure, robust, and comply with legislative requirements in the proper maintenance of critical software; in fact, a large part of the Microsoft DevOps lifecycle was used to maintain Windows and other Microsoft critical products, using their own software to evolve the platform. Eventually, Microsoft started to open their platform with a free tier of operation and make it available to all developers, although at that time the documentation wasn't great and setting up automation was a very gruesome task.

Fast forward to today and all the history that went into making a robust automation platform is well oiled, easy to adopt, and has a large community of developers contributing extensions to further expand the capabilities of the platform.

Costs Involved

At a basic level, Microsoft has ensured there is a completely free option for any developer or company to adopt their DevOps platform. Reach beyond that and you will need to pay for ongoing operations, but thankfully there is a wide gap before you get there.

Where costs do start to get involved, it comes down to the hosting needed to run your pipelines (the machine your builds run on), from hosted virtual servers giving you a slice of operation among many to dedicated machines, virtual or physical depending on the demands for your operations. However, Azure also provides you with the option to also use your own hardware by installing an "Agent" and using that to run intensive workloads; you can even mix and match if you wish, running some cheaper operations on the free Microsoft hosting and only using your own hardware for intensive workloads.

Free tier: The free tier includes the following aspects:

- First five users free (Basic license)

- Azure Pipelines

    - One Microsoft-hosted CI/CD (one concurrent job, up to 30 hours per month)

    - One self-hosted CI/CD concurrent job

- Azure Boards – Work item tracking and Kanban boards

- Azure Repos – Unlimited private Git repos

- Azure Artifacts – Two GiB free per organization

If you exceed the 30 hours, you essentially pay for an extra block of 30 hours (additional parallel jobs) for the month you use it for, which stands at $40 per month per 30 hours (1800 minutes).

Check the Azure Pipelines Billing calculator for any additional costs beyond the free offerings mentioned earlier.

Comparison

Table 3-2 shows a comparison of the standard features in automation as it pertains to Azure Pipelines.

Table 3-2. *Comparing standard automation features pertaining to Azure Pipelines*

Feature	Level of Support	Simplicity	Critical Notes
Source Control Integration	Azure, Bitbucket, GitHub, GitHub Enterprise, Git generic, Subversion	Fully driven UI for integration	Connects to practically any source service available
Self-Hosting	Yes, Mac, Windows, and Linux	Clear documentation for setup, although can take a few attempts to get right	Make sure to use a dedicated "Build" user for the authentication, do not use personal accounts
Custom Pipelines	Yes, including a marketplace of pre-build integrations	Built-in editor in the Web interface	Remember to use the resources you need in the pipeline, and do not stay stuck with any one OS
Unity Project Building	Yes, through marketplace extension or build it yourself through script	Marketplace add-ons make this very easy, a bit trickier building manually	Make sure to lean on the strong shoulders of the community and learn from them
Build Distribution	Yes, but requires security configuration	Links are autogenerated for use	The trick is that Azure is a secure platform, so testers need access to the links. Projects can be public to make it easier if possible
Packaging	Yes, through Azure Artifacts (max 2 GB free tier)	Easy	Make sure to manage clearing out old builds that are not required to keep storage down

(continued)

Table 3-2. (*continued*)

Feature	Level of Support	Simplicity	Critical Notes
Deployment	Yes, through AppCenter or TestFlight integration	AppCenter is straightforward, Apple takes some work	Make sure to include all the necessary steps in the pipeline for deployment, including distributing secret keys and certificates
Analytics	Yes, through AppCenter	Fairly easy	Azure pipelines do give basic build statistics, but AppCenter provides better in-app analytics
Other Integrations	Yes, through custom scripts or marketplace extensions	Hardest part is choosing the right plugin/script to meet your requirements	Like with anything, remember KISS and do not go overboard, add only what adds value to your pipeline. But do experiment!

Personal Comments

While you can use Azure pipelines exclusively, I find it best to focus on what Azure Pipelines is best at, by creating and managing builds, including the distribution of builds; it is primarily what it was built for. For simpler tasks, I do tend to use other services (such as GitHub Actions) for the quick and dirty tasks to manage day-to-day operations. Azure can do it all if you need it to, but I find it best to balance things and use the free tiers and their power where it is needed.

GitHub Actions

GitHub has long been one of the best git source control hosts available for some time, even before its acquisition by Microsoft. But once Microsoft acquired GitHub, we saw a rapid upscale in the capabilities being offered, and one of the most important of these was the development of GitHub Actions. GitHub Actions has grown in strength since that time, seen by many to be the reinventing of the older Azure pipelines capabilities but for a more open source crowd (in fact, it should come as no surprise that the list of Microsoft-hosted agents available to GitHub mirrors the ones used by Azure pipelines exactly).

The community has jumped on the openness of GitHub actions, and there are now many more extensions (custom actions) available for GitHub than what is available with Azure; however, this does have to come with a pinch of salt as anyone can host an Action on a repository, and you need to be more careful with what public actions you consume to ensure they are ONLY doing what you need them to do and nothing else (although Microsoft has really beefed up security on GitHub of late, identifying any repositories or code that is intended to be malicious and warning you via weekly reports).

The barrier to entry is also a lot lower on GitHub, as all you need is the repository and nothing else, no complicated setup as with Azure, with the only trade-off being that it is only usable by GitHub and not any other source control provider.

Bitbucket and GitLab also have their own offerings with similar capabilities based on their own platform strengths; however, the terminology is the same, so learning one, like GitHub Actions, will set you in good stead for all.

Costs Involved

As with almost anything to do with GitHub, everything is free, to a point, although you only really start paying once your development team gets bigger (more than five members). The free tier includes a LOT:

- Unlimited repositories, public and private

- 2000 GitHub actions minutes per month

- 500 MB package storage

And much more.

Once you exceed these, you effectively pay by the hour for additional usage:

- $0.48 per hour – Linux

- $0.96 per hour – Windows

- $4.80 per hour – Mac (woah)

See Figure 3-2 for details.

Figure 3-2. *GitHub Actions pricing*

Obviously, these prices are for Microsoft-hosted agents only; self-hosted is still free, always.

Comparison

Table 3-3 shows a comparison of the standard features in automation as it pertains to GitHub Actions.

Table 3-3. *Comparing standard automation features pertaining to GitHub actions*

Feature	Level of Support	Simplicity	Critical Notes
Source Control Integration	GitHub only	As easy as creating a repository	
Self-Hosting	Yes	Even easier than Azure	As with Azure, make sure to use a dedicated user for automation
Custom Pipelines	Yes, including a marketplace of pre-build integrations	Easy to adopt	Just make sure the actions are well reviewed, or build your own
Unity Project Building	Yes, through manual scripts or Community extensions	Easy'ish	Best to use Self-Hosting for building Unity, although there are marketplace actions to do it for you
Build Distribution	Yes, through custom scripts	Very accessible	Just watch your free limits
Packaging	Yes, provided users have access to the repository	Very accessible	Just watch your free limits
Deployment	Yes, through manual scripts or Community extensions	Very accessible	
Analytics	Only GitHub, app analytics can be provided through AppCenter or integration	Most vendors provide GitHub instructions	
Other Integrations	Yes, through manual scripts or Community extensions	Very easy	

Personal Comments

GitHub actions have now become my go-to provider for automation on my projects, especially if the source is already on GitHub; there is just so much flexibility you can do almost anything. Microsoft has also not been sitting still either, and they add new features on a regular basis, especially the new "Dependabot" features which monitor not just your code but also any code linked to your project through actions or submodules, always pays to know your project is safe (or you are at least aware of issues). I expect GitHub actions to continue to grow as the platform evolves and the community provides even more tools beyond even what Microsoft provides.

Summary

We have now set the stage and given you a list of the products covered by this title; next up, we will dig through the terminology and technology employed by automation and how it applies to building your Unity project before then jumping into setting up each service.

Onward.

CHAPTER 4

The Structure of Automation

Like any technology, automation has its own particular language, ways, and means, although thankfully most of the industry has settled on standard terms to describe similar behaviors and patterns, so in learning one you can easily and quickly adapt it to any other.

The big exception to this is Unity Gaming Services, as they do not offer a standard pattern for automation and require you to Code in Unity to customize it; it stands alone. Not to say it is bad, just that investments in this type of automation are very specific and sometimes difficult to adapt should you need to apply anything other than what Unity gives you "out of the box". It has its uses and can often be the "quick approach" while you work on customizing something specific to your business.

In this chapter, I will detail all the relevant terms and notations used by automation and then finish with a brief walk-through on how we build out automation configuration using what you have learned.

© Simon Jackson 2023
S. Jackson, *Accelerating Unity Through Automation*, https://doi.org/10.1007/978-1-4842-9508-3_4

The Speech of Automation

What follows is a simple breakdown of each term used in automation and in layman's terms, showing what they really mean. The documentation provided by vendors does a decent job, but I have always found it slightly lacking as it often talks around subjects or expects you to know "other things" before having read them. Here is a list of all the critical terms.

Actions

Actions in GitHub Actions terminology is an individual operation or a self-contained workflow for use by automation, also called an Extension in Azure Pipelines. These are reusable automations that can be consumed by an individual Step in a job.

GitHub Actions can come from scripts internal to the repository (also called reusable workflows) or from other GitHub repositories (which are public). While all the GitHub-owned actions are considered safe, care must be taken with other freely available actions to ensure they are a good fit as there are likely to be many variations published; check the reviews/comments and issues against the repository for any GitHub Actions (or Azure Pipelines extension in the Azure Extensions Marketplace) so that you understand its use. It is also recommended to do a few searches about new actions to see what the general developer consensus is for any individual action.

Like any other public GitHub repository, there may also be Forks (managed copies) of an action where a developer has extended the capabilities of an Action or continued to support it beyond the original developer's design. It is a world of choice, so shop around when you need your automation to do something new and take the time to research those options.

References

- `https://github.com/marketplace?type=actions`

Agent/Runner

An Agent (also referred to as a Runner) denotes an operational environment needed to run an automation. It can be an entire machine/PC or simply a service running on a machine (usually several). In the case of self-hosted agents, which are run on your own hardware and can have multiple agents running on the same machine (provided it can run them all). In the case of hosted agents, this is either a virtual machine provided by the vendor or a container running in a virtual environment.

In all cases, when an automation is run on an agent, its environment is cleaned up so as not to contaminate builds with the results from a previous run (this can be overridden if needed for continuous builds).

References

- GitHub-hosted agents

  `https://docs.github.com/en/actions/using-github-hosted-runners/about-github-hosted-runners`

- GitHub self-hosted

  `https://docs.github.com/en/actions/hosting-your-own-runners/about-self-hosted-runners`

- Azure Runners

  `https://learn.microsoft.com/en-us/azure/devops/pipelines/agents/agents`

See Chapter 5 about choosing where to host your agents.

Approvals

For mission-critical workflows, there may be cases where an individual (or team) needs to approve the progression of an automation from one stage to another, often called gated workflows/approvals. These "stops" will halt the automation until the approval is given (usually in the web interface) before progressing to the next step. This is used to verify all checks have been made procedurally for a production release or before committing costly resources for an operation (using Cloud-hosted billable time).

There is no right or wrong way to approach these; take care that they meet the business needs so as not to hold up normal operations.

References

- Azure Pipelines approvals

  `https://learn.microsoft.com/en-us/azure/devops/pipelines/process/approvals`

- GitHub "Manual Approval" custom action

  `https://trstringer.com/github-actions-manual-approval/`

Note   Approvals are not built-in by default to GitHub Actions, so you will need to use a custom action to implement them, as shown earlier.

Artifact/Package

Both GitHub and Azure provide a "staging location" where finished builds and/or assets can be published once an automation is complete, whether the automation was successful or not. If a build fails, then logs can be uploaded; if the build is successful, then a zip of the test build can be made available for testers to download, or simply publish a report on the testing. The "staging" area can also be used to share information between builds, such as the last successful build version number, or random keys/seeds used in the build, or even a background configuration file that is used to change the build as it works through the system.

Ultimately, it is a secure area used by a build; however, it is specific to an automation run on a single host and is NOT shared, so if you need to share information across multiple hosts, then you will need an alternate solution.

References

- GitHub Packages

  `https://docs.github.com/en/actions/publishing-packages/about-packaging-with-github-actions`

- Azure Artifacts

  `https://learn.microsoft.com/en-us/azure/devops/artifacts/start-using-azure-artifacts`

Azure Pipelines

Azure Pipelines is Microsoft's offering in the Automation/DevOps (Developer Operations) space powered by Microsoft Azure. It is also linked with Microsoft's other Azure offerings, including

- Azure Boards (project management)

- Azure Repos (source control)

- Test Plans (automation test reporting)

- Artifacts

References

- `https://azure.microsoft.com/en-gb/products/devops/pipelines/`

Branch

A branch is a source control term related to a named checkpoint in code. Each repository has a default branch (normally called "main") and can contain any number of other branches containing changes based on the default branch, for example, a development branch which has everything that is currently being updated and changed since the last release. It is important to note that all automation will work on a single branch in the code, to test/build upon that code in isolation, effectively checking the work "as it stands."

In a normal release pipeline, you would have the following branches:

- The "Main" branch contains the currently published build.

- A "Development" branch, based on the "Main" branch, contains all changes that have been made since the last release.

- "Feature" branches contain individual batches of changes to be proposed for inclusion in the development branch.

In any properly maintained release pipeline, work is built in isolation and submitted (via a "Pull Request") to its parent branch before being accepted and "merged." This flows through until the development branch has reached a milestone where it is ready to be published again and another "Pull Request" is made from the "development" branch to the "main" branch, to reset the process and start work on the next release. This is all optional of course and a lot of projects simply use a single "main" branch and push all changes directly to the main branch continually, especially with smaller Proof of Concept (POC) projects; however, you lose any kind of change control or reporting by bypassing a fuller process. Whichever you use, you will need to take this into account while building your automation.

References

- `https://learngitbranching.js.org/`

Comment

Comments are a powerful and mostly underused feature in automation. If a team is working on a source control project, they can make comments against changes or pending pull requests, useful for communicating around the code. However, it can also be read by the automation and used to alter the flow of the automation using those comments; in the most common scenarios, reserved keywords like "Build" or "Check Build" are used to enact additional automation jobs/steps or simply ask the automation pipeline to "rerun" the workflow again automatically.

References

- https://docs.github.com/en/pull-requests/collaborating-
  with-pull-requests/reviewing-changes-in-pull-requests/
  commenting-on-a-pull-request

Conditions

Conditions in a workflow are expressions that are used to determine if a Job or Step "should" run, for example, "if the current branch is 'Development,' then run additional jobs/steps in the automation." The expressions can be based on almost anything; for more details, see the "Conditionals" section.

References

- GitHub Actions

  https://docs.github.com/en/actions/using-jobs/using-conditions-
  to-control-job-execution

- Azure Pipelines

  https://learn.microsoft.com/en-us/azure/devops/pipelines/
  process/conditions

Container

Containerized delivery is a modern term for deploying solutions in today's applications; effectively, a container is an isolated space built on a server with a preconfigured environment defined, for example, a Unix server with several applications preinstalled and a defined operating environment. Containers can also be used in automation to provide a specific definition for an agent to run in a particular way that is always clean, with an expected configuration, màking it easier to test the deployment of software. (The GameCI GitHub actions use this method; see Chapter 11 for more details.)

References

- https://learn.microsoft.com/en-us/dotnet/architecture/
  microservices/container-docker-introduction/

Continuous Delivery

Continuous delivery relates to the automated pattern of creating builds and publishing them to a resource for testing, whether it is an automated deployment environment such as Apple's TestFlight, Microsoft's AppCenter, or simply providing an application to install from a published folder for testers to build from. Extended versions of continuous delivery also include UX/UI testing through automated robots (machine learning that can replicate human input on a screen) and deliver test results from a running application.

References

- https://azure.microsoft.com/en-us/overview/continuous-
  delivery-vs-continuous-deployment/

Continuous Integration

Continuous integration relates to the processes used in automation to test and validate code/functionality prior to a build, checking that standards and practices have been followed and running automated code tests to ensure the expected results are output based on the latest changes (ensuring the code ran the same as it did before the changes and outputting the same results). In the more complex continuous integration processes, external real-world or mock data is also used to validate the correct operation of the application using the information that will be normally consumed by the application when running, a precheck before an actual build is made.

References

- https://learn.microsoft.com/en-us/devops/develop/what-is-continuous-integration

Deployment

Any process whereby the output or results from an automation run are published to a resource (a folder or site) is regarded as a deployment – normally a singular area where testers and those wishing to install the application can find the builds.

Deployment Group

Deployment groups are a collection of users for whom builds are made available, usually used for security reasons to ensure the correct people have access to specific builds, for example, alpha testers can access all builds, beta testers can access only beta and retail builds, public testers can test public betas and retail, and so on.

References

- https://learn.microsoft.com/en-us/azure/devops/pipelines/release/deployment-groups

Environment

An environment relates to the working environment for an automation which is specific to the machine the automation is running on. Environments can also access environment parameters which can either be specific to the host or inherited from the automation setup, with variables and secrets provided from the organization, project, or even the specific workflow run.

Event

An event is a hook or condition you can use to trigger an automation, such as a Pull Request, a Push, or even a comment. Events are specific to the vendor platform that an automation is operating from but are usually quite extensive based on the API that the vendor operates.

See the additional links for the lists of events offered by Azure and GitHub.

References

- GitHub events

  https://docs.github.com/en/actions/using-workflows/events-that-trigger-workflows

- Azure Pipelines events

  https://learn.microsoft.com/en-us/azure/devops/pipelines/build/triggers

GitHub Actions

GitHub Actions are GitHub's answer to automation, evolved from Azure pipelines and similar to Bitbucket workflows; they offer increasing support for the most complex automation loads, as well as offering community support for additional workflows/extensions through its GitHub Actions Marketplace.

References

- https://docs.github.com/en/actions

Job/Jobs

A Job relates to a collection of activities (steps) to be performed in an automation run; each Job is contained within a single "Jobs" group in a workflow definition. Jobs can be organized by activity (Build, Test, Report, etc.) or be defined to only run under certain conditions (branch == development). How you break up individual workflow definitions is down to the person maintaining the automation, and there is no right/wrong way to implement them. You can either

- Have separate workflow definitions, each containing a single job to run based on the state of the repository.

- Or you can have a single workflow definition with many jobs, all set to run depending on conditions.

The choice is up to you; personally, I prefer to have several workflow definitions with a limited number of Jobs to make maintenance of the workflow easier.

References

- GitHub Actions Jobs

  `https://docs.github.com/en/actions/using-jobs`

- Azure Pipelines Jobs

  `https://learn.microsoft.com/en-us/azure/devops/pipelines/process/phases`

Library

The library is the area in a vendor's implementation that stores and maintains environment variables and secrets. On Azure, this is maintained in the "**LIBRARY**" tab of a Pipeline; on GitHub, it is defined within the GitHub Actions "**SECRETS AND VARIABLES**" configuration settings.

References

- `https://learn.microsoft.com/en-us/azure/devops/pipelines/library`

Mac Host

Hosts come in all shapes and sizes and differ based on the operating system requirements for a host; in this case, it refers to a Macintosh Build host running on MacOS which is required for building any applications for iOS-based clients such as iPhone, iPad, or Mac. Mac can also be used for building Android applications.

Parameters/Variables

Parameters are additional settings that are provided to individual actions, such as specifying a required version number, a state, or secret key that is required for the Action to run. Always check the documentation for the Action as to what parameters are needed to run it. Parameters can be mandatory or optional depending on their use.

Pipeline/Workflow

A pipeline is the Azure definition for an individual automation workflow, containing the operations required for the automation to run. On Azure, each pipeline needs to be declared through the UI and associated with an individual pipeline YAML file located in the source code repository where the automation is going to run against.

Note   The branch the YAML file is located in is important; by default, it will use the automation definition from the default branch of the repository, but it will use the YAML definition from the branch it is run on when the pipeline is executed. If the YAML file in the default branch is different to the branch the automation is running on, it will use the configuration from the target branch; keep this in mind if you are changing what the automation does between builds.

References

- GitHub Actions workflows

  ```
  https://docs.github.com/en/actions/using-workflows
  ```

- Azure Pipelines creation

  ```
  https://learn.microsoft.com/en-us/azure/devops/pipelines/create-
  first-pipeline
  ```

Pull Request

A Pull Request is a source control term related to making a task to pull code from one branch and merge it into another (comparing the differences and adding the changes to the base branch).

A normal source workflow is as follows:

- The "**Development**" branch has the current stage of development.

- A "**Feature**" branch is created to make changes to development; once complete, a "**Pull Request**" is made to take the changes from the feature branch and update them into the "Development" branch.

- The "**Pull Request**" is then reviewed, and if accepted, the Pull Request is merged (copied into the base branch "development"), and then the "feature" branch is closed to clean up.

- "**Development**" has now been updated with the additional changes.

"**Pull Requests**" are good practice for maintaining where code is changed and by whom in a project, although it is completely optional and some developers still just make changes directly to the base branch, rather than creating a new branch and then "pulling" them in later.

References

- https://docs.github.com/en/pull-requests/collaborating-with-pull-requests/proposing-changes-to-your-work-with-pull-requests/creating-a-pull-request

Push/Pull

When using source control, there are effectively two copies of your project, one on the server and one on your PC (or several PCs if you are brave).

- When you want to copy the current state on the server (including any branches) to your local PC, this is called a "Pull."

- When you want to push the changes from your PC to the server, this is called a "Push."

In most cases, everything will work fine; the only issue that can occur is if there are changes on BOTH the server AND your PC which can prevent you from pushing your latest changes; luckily, you can still pull the changes from the server again to update your local copy and then push your new updates back to the server, although if the changes were made to the same file, you will need to fix any "merge errors" manually by opening the files and updating them to the state you want.

References

- https://github.com/git-guides/git-pull

- https://github.com/git-guides/git-push

Run

When code and automation meet, this becomes a run. In short, runs are individual executions of a workflow on a specific branch of your repository; once running, you cannot change anything (else, it would invalidate the run). You can rerun a workflow/pipeline, but it will be under the exact same conditions that the first run was performed under (any changes you make to the source or the workflow will have no effect); this is normally done if the host the pipeline was running on had issues and they have now been resolved (e.g., ran out of disk space, had the wrong version, or no version of Unity installed).

Normally, you run the automation and it works have a party; if it fails, look at the logs for the run and make changes and then execute the workflow again in a new run.

References

- GitHub Actions run reports

  ```
  https://docs.github.com/en/actions/monitoring-and-troubleshooting-
  workflows/viewing-workflow-run-history
  ```

- Azure Pipelines run reports

  ```
  https://learn.microsoft.com/en-us/azure/devops/pipelines/
  process/runs
  ```

Runner/Host

The Runner or host simply relates to a specific Agent running on a physical or virtual host (hosts can support multiple agents). Each runner can operate a single automation run at a time, but multiple runners can be used by a single automation where it has concurrent jobs defined.

Stage

Stages defined in an automation workflow configuration are the gated elements where something is usually required before progressing to the next stage, normally associated with approvals. This might indicate automation that is for development, then QA, and finally Test/Build. Not mandatory for most automation workflows, but they can be added if you need to implement approvals in your workflow.

References

- Stages are unique to Azure (but can be implemented in a slightly different way in GitHub Actions)

   https://learn.microsoft.com/en-us/azure/devops/pipelines/
   process/stages

Step/Steps/Task

A Step (also known as Task in Azure pipelines) relates to a single activity within a workflow Job, such as checking our code or running a script. Steps are grouped under a single "Steps" group within a single job.

Trigger

A trigger is defined as the set of requirements or things that need to happen for a workflow to be automatically enacted, such as when a Pull Request is made or when code is pushed to a branch. Other triggers will depend on the available events that are exposed by the vendor, such as comment triggers and scheduled triggers (run workflow every XX seconds).

Normally, to run an automation manually (especially on GitHub), a workflow needs to declare it can be run manually before the UI will allow it to be manually executed, called a "manual trigger."

References

- GitHub Actions triggers

  https://docs.github.com/en/actions/using-workflows/triggering-a-workflow

- Azure pipelines triggers

  https://learn.microsoft.com/en-us/azure/devops/pipelines/build/triggers

Ubuntu (Linux) Host

Hosts come in all shapes and sizes and differ based on the operating system requirements for a host; in this case, it refers to a Linux Build host usually running a Linux distribution such as Ubuntu; this is required for building any applications for Linux-based servers and clients. Linux hosts are more commonly used for automation tasks such as validation or tests where a specific operating system is not needed as Linux is commonly faster and cheaper for simpler operations. In a lot of cases, Linux hosts are used for most automations, using only a specific operating system host for client builds, using what is most efficient for the specific operation or task required. Comment validation automation normally runs on Linux since it does not even need access to the code, for example.

Windows Host

Hosts come in all shapes and sizes and differ based on the operating system requirements for a host; in this case, it refers to a Windows Build host running on a Windows Server or client which is required for building any applications for Windows clients and UWP; Windows can also be used for building Android applications.

Workflow/Pipeline

Workflow/pipeline relates to a single script used for an automation, containing all the setup, Jobs, and Steps required for a workflow to run with predefined triggers to call the workflow into action. It can also be configured to run manually in the automation interface.

References

- GitHub Actions workflow syntax

  ```
  https://docs.github.com/en/actions/using-workflows/workflow-
  syntax-for-github-actions
  ```

- Azure Pipelines workflow editor

  ```
  https://learn.microsoft.com/en-us/azure/devops/pipelines/get-
  started/yaml-pipeline-editor
  ```

Yaml/yml

YAML (yml for short) is the language in which automation is written; most automation hosts have standardized the terms/references for producing automation workflows written in YAML. Take note of the "Formatting" section, which outlines YAML's need for fixed spacing for defining Jobs and Steps, very critical.

References

- Standards definition

  `https://en.wikipedia.org/wiki/YAML`

- GitHub implementation

  `https://docs.github.com/en/actions/creating-actions/metadata-syntax-for-github-actions`

- Azure implementation

  `https://learn.microsoft.com/en-us/azure/devops/pipelines/yaml-schema`

The First Look at Automation Configuration

The core of any automation configuration centers around the list of things you want your automation to achieve; there is some preamble you can set to control how often your automation runs, define defaults for which server runs the entire operation, and whether automation can be manually run, but these are usually specific to the vendor's implementation.

Focusing on the actual work, the following script is an example of a workflow YAML definition:

```
name: your-first-workflow
run-name: ${{ github.actor }} is learning automation
on: [push]
jobs:
  my-first-workflow:
    runs-on: ubuntu-latest
    steps:
      - uses: actions/checkout@v3
      - uses: actions/setup-node@v3
        with:
          node-version: '14'
      - id: run-script
        name: 'This is what my step is called'
        run: |
            echo 'My first ever script has been run'
        shell: pwsh
```

Figure 4-1. *First workflow example*

For simplicity, we will be using **GitHub Actions** for the examples; however, Azure Pipelines is very similar.

Breaking this down, we can easily identify the sections that define our automation script.

1. The Name of the Automation

```
name: your-first-workflow
```

Each automation needs a name; this is what is used to uniquely identify the operation and what is displayed in the GUI for the automation as well as logs and such. The name must be a single lowercase definition with no spaces or special characters. However, we can also provide the name a "**Display Name**" using a run-name tag to have a more friendly description displayed should you so wish (which I always find helpful):

```
run-name: ${{ github.actor }} is learning automation
```

You can also see that a script parameter (github.actor) has been used in this case to make it dynamic, in this case, showing the name of the user who initiated the automation. This is completely optional but does help provide a more friendly description to tell readers what the automation is for.

See the "Secrets and Environment Variables" section later in this chapter for more information on these variables.

---

2. The Primary Trigger for the Automation

Triggers are events that occur on the vendor platform that automation can attach to in order to start the operation; in this case, the script is listening for ANY Push events (when code is checked into the repository the automation is running on):

```
on: [push]
```

Any **Push** to the source control repository will enact the automation and run the work. Other options generally include Pull Requests, comments, and more, all depending on what API events the vendor provides.

3. The "Jobs" Section

The **Jobs** section is a group header in the automation configuration, and **there can only be one**; an automation script can contain many jobs, each with its own specific conditions, actions, and steps, but there can only be one Jobs section:

```
jobs:
```

4. Individual Job Definitions

This is where the magic starts to happen; you can have many jobs within an automation workflow, although you will most likely only ever have one. If you have multiple, it is normally where you want different things to happen in a workflow depending on the state, branch, or event that caused the workflow to run, such as having an additional job run because an author used a specific message in their commit message like "Publish Release."

```
my-first-workflow:
  runs-on: ubuntu-latest
```

You can also see earlier that as part of the job definition, the configuration states which **agent** the job should be run on (Ubuntu/Linux in this case); this can be set in the automation preamble to have all the jobs run on the same host; however, it is a more common practice to set the running host "per job" so that work can be run concurrently, having multiple jobs running on multiple agents at the same time.

5. The "Steps" Section

The same as the "Jobs" section, within each job there is a section to group together the **Steps** that are executed to complete the job; again, **there can only be one** per job (obviously, there can be several throughout the whole automation script but only ONE per Job section):

```
steps:
```

From here, the real work begins for what the automation script is intended to do.

6. Individual Step Definitions

Steps can take several forms. The "uses:" statement indicates that an external script or reusable function is to be used as a single step:

```
- uses: actions/checkout@v3
```

or manually created steps intended to either run a script or pre-built function:

```
- id: run-script
  name: 'This is what my step is called'
  run:
```

Both are interchangeable between steps, but only one pattern can be used at a time; trying to use the "uses" statement when you have preceded it with an "id" or another command will simply result in error.

Use examples and other references when building out your steps to ensure you are executing a SINGLE thing in each step.

Individual steps compare to a set of instructions:

- Do this.

- Then this.

- Finally, do this.

These will all then run on the host or agent determined by the **Job** definition.

Take Care For a step to run, you must ensure everything that is needed for a Step to execute **MUST** be available on the host prior to running a step; you cannot install something on the host that is required while a step is running. If a component, feature, or piece of software is needed (for instance, NodeJS), then a preceding step should check and/or install that dependency BEFORE a step is due to run. In the example, NodeJS is installed using the actions/setup-node@v3 step, which prepares the host for using NPM.

We covered the kinds of things that can be executed in a step in Chapter 2, listing out a few of the multitude of operations that can be performed by automation.

7. Step Parameters

Some workflow steps also require additional parameters to function; this can be anything from settings to the most common usage, secrets (phrases, keys, or secure items). Parameters for Steps are denoted with the "**with**" argument, as follows:

```
- uses: actions/setup-node@v3
  with:
    node-version: '14'
```

The preceding parameter informs the "**setup-node**" action that "**Version 14**" is specifically needed when installing NodeJS. Some parameters are optional, some are mandatory, so check the documentation for the action or extension for details of what is required. Sometimes, if you are REALLY lucky, the action you are consuming will include examples to help you along and copy (just make sure the parameters make sense for your automation!), for example, the checkout action (likely the most used GitHub Actions):

```
https://github.com/actions/checkout
```

GitHub "Checkout" comes with extensive documentation/example configuration:

```
- uses: actions/checkout@v3
  with:
    # Repository name with owner. For example, actions/checkout
    # Default: ${{ github.repository }}
    repository: ''

    # The branch, tag or SHA to checkout. When checking out the repository that
    # triggered a workflow, this defaults to the reference or SHA for that event.
    # Otherwise, uses the default branch.
    ref: ''

    # Personal access token (PAT) used to fetch the repository. The PAT is configured
    # with the local git config, which enables your scripts to run authenticated git
    # commands. The post-job step removes the PAT.
    #
    # We recommend using a service account with the least permissions necessary. Also
    # when generating a new PAT, select the least scopes necessary.
    #
    # [Learn more about creating and using encrypted
secrets](https://help.github.com/en/actions/automating-your-workflow-with-github-
actions/creating-and-using-encrypted-secrets)
    #
    # Default: ${{ github.token }}
    token: ''

    # SSH key used to fetch the repository. The SSH key is configured with the local
    # git config, which enables your scripts to run authenticated git commands. The
    # post-job step removes the SSH key.
    #
    # We recommend using a service account with the least permissions necessary.
    #
    # [Learn more about creating and using encrypted
secrets](https://help.github.com/en/actions/automating-your-workflow-with-github-
actions/creating-and-using-encrypted-secrets)
    ssh-key: ''
```

Figure 4-2. *GitHub Checkout examples*

```
# Known hosts in addition to the user and global host key database. The public SSH
# keys for a host may be obtained using the utility `ssh-keyscan`. For example,
# `ssh-keyscan github.com`. The public key for github.com is always implicitly
# added.
ssh-known-hosts: ''

# Whether to perform strict host key checking. When true, adds the options
# `StrictHostKeyChecking=yes` and `CheckHostIP=no` to the SSH command line. Use
# the input `ssh-known-hosts` to configure additional hosts.
# Default: true
ssh-strict: ''

# Whether to configure the token or SSH key with the local git config
# Default: true
persist-credentials: ''

# Relative path under $GITHUB_WORKSPACE to place the repository
path: ''

# Whether to execute `git clean -ffdx && git reset --hard HEAD` before fetching
# Default: true
clean: ''

# Number of commits to fetch. 0 indicates all history for all branches and tags.
# Default: 1
fetch-depth: ''

# Whether to download Git-LFS files
# Default: false
lfs: ''

# Whether to checkout submodules: `true` to checkout submodules or `recursive` to
# recursively checkout submodules.
#
# When the `ssh-key` input is not provided, SSH URLs beginning with
# `git@github.com:` are converted to HTTPS.
#
# Default: false
submodules: ''

# Add repository path as safe.directory for Git global config by running `git
```

Figure 4-2. (*continued*)

```
# config --global --add safe.directory <path>`
# Default: true
set-safe-directory: "

# The base URL for the GitHub instance that you are trying to clone from, will use
# environment defaults to fetch from the same instance that the workflow is
# running from unless specified. Example URLs are https://github.com or
# https://my-ghes-server.example.com
github-server-url: "
```

Figure 4-2. (*continued*)

This includes a fantastic amount of example use cases with clear descriptions for what each parameter does; have a read yourself and see.

Formatting

One critical thing to understand with automation scripting is formatting! The script is governed by the layout and spacing between each section, for example:

- The Name, On, and Jobs sections listed as follows have NO preceding spaces; they are always to the far left in the configuration file.

- Each single Job definition is indented by at least two spaces (two spaces is the expected default).

- Any arguments for the job are then further indented by an additional two spaces, such as runs-on and the Steps group (four spaces in total).

- Individual steps are then indented another two spaces (six spaces in total).

- Arguments/parameters for individual steps are then finally indented an additional two spaces (eight spaces or two tabs).

Here is the previous example again for reference with "." added to denote spaces:

```
name: your-first-workflow
run-name: ${{ github.actor }} is learning automation
on: [push]
jobs:
..my-first-workflow:
....runs-on: ubuntu-latest
....steps:
......- uses: actions/checkout@v3
......- uses: actions/setup-node@v3
........with:
..........node-version: '14'
......- id: run-script
........name: 'This is what my step is called'
........run: |
........   echo 'My first ever script has been run'
........shell: pwsh
```

Figure 4-3. *YAML formatting example*

THE SPACING IS CRUCIAL, as this notation is understood and required by the automation interpreters; learn it well to save a multitude of debugging and head-scratching hours as to why your automation fails to load or simply reports a "**formatting error**" with the configuration. Better yet, use tools like VSCode with the document format set to "YAML" to better highlight your configuration and learn what is not formatted correctly. Azure Pipelines also includes a visual editor and will highlight problems early.

Secrets and Environment Variables

The last thing you want in any automation script are variables that are likely to change frequently or information which is in essence "**SECRET**" (like API keys and passwords); thankfully, most vendor platform services provide the ability to set information at either the environmental level or from a secret encrypted store, both outside the contents of your actual workflow. Additionally, most automation providers also allow you to define fixed variables within the automation scripts themselves for less frequently changed configuration, but in all honesty, I have always looked to use methods I can maintain outside of the automation script to avoid repeated changes to the automation itself.

Ideally, automation scripts should be a FIXED thing, only needing to be changed when the conditions or requirements of the automation change; that way, the changes can be tracked effectively. Changing individual values is not very efficient.

The only real difference between environment variables and secrets is that secrets are considered secure and once entered cannot be read again (by a human at least) and attempts to "print" them out in automation will fail; secrets are shared secretly and never exposed where environment variables are open, even in logs.

Both secrets and environment variables can generally be declared for either the entire organization or for a single project; in fact, some providers also allow for them to be set for individual workflows, although this is not used as much. Generally speaking, **VARIABLES** and **SECRETS** are set at an organisational level and reused across all repositories unless there is a specific reason for a single project to behave differently.

Environment variables are accessed as follows:

```
${{ env.MY_VARIABLE }}
```

whereas secrets are accessed very specifically:

```
${{ secrets.SuperSecret }}
```

In GitHub actions (and Azure), there are also a set of built-in environment variables that are available to describe the environment that the workflow is being run in, for example, see Table 4-1.

Table 4-1. *GitHub environment variables*

Variable	Description
GITHUB_ACTION_ PATH	The path where an action is located. This property is only supported in composite actions. You can use this path to access files located in the same repository as the action. For example, */home/runner/work/_actions/repo-owner/ name-of-action-repo/v1*
GITHUB_ACTION_ REPOSITORY	For a step executing an action, this is the owner and repository name of the action. For example, *actions/checkout*
GITHUB_ACTIONS	Always set to true when GitHub Actions is running the workflow. You can use this variable to differentiate when tests are being run locally or by GitHub Actions
GITHUB_ACTOR	The name of the person or app that initiated the workflow. For example, *octocat*
GITHUB_ACTOR_ ID	The account ID of the person or app that triggered the initial workflow run. For example, *1234567* Note that this is different from the actor username

For more details on the different built-in environment variables for the vendors covered in this title, check their documentation pages here:

- GitHub

    https://docs.github.com/en/actions/learn-github-actions/
    variables#default-environment-variables

- Azure

    https://learn.microsoft.com/en-us/azure/devops/pipelines/build/
    variables

In the working examples to be demonstrated for each solution later in this title, I will demonstrate setting up and using secrets as part of the setup, using the most common scenario, creating a secure access token to use in the workflow.

Conditionals

Almost every aspect of the automation pipeline supports conditional statements; these are used to determine whether or not a workflow, job, or step should run and can be used to great effect, such as only running a publish task when changes are committed to the "Main" branch for release or doing additional checks and balances when "development" is updated.

Care should always be taken when introducing a conditional test in any workflow, ideally setting up a clean or clone repository to test that you meet the conditions in the right way when the workflow actually runs. The last thing you want is to get the conditional wrong or inverted on live code. **ALWAYS** test workflows in a nondestructive repository!

Conditionals use basic expressions to denote what should happen when, for example:

```
if: github.repository == 'octo-org/octo-repo-prod'
```

This condition uses the GitHub environment variable (as mentioned earlier) of "github.repository" and tests to see if the organization and repository names match "octo-org/octo-repo-prod". If so, the Job/Step the conditional is attached to will execute, and if not, it will be skipped, simple.

Listing 4-1 shows the full example from GitHub.

Listing 4-1. GitHub Checkout example

```
name: example-workflow
on: [push]
jobs:
  production-deploy:
    if: github.repository == 'octo-org/octo-repo-prod'
    runs-on: ubuntu-latest
    steps:
      - uses: actions/checkout@v3
      - uses: actions/setup-node@v3
        with:
          node-version: '14'
      - run: npm install -g bats
```

Although this conditional statement "can" be used at the Step level, it is recommended to only use it for Jobs, to keep the workflow clearer on what it is doing and why.

Job Output

When the job runs and the steps are executed, you will get a lengthy report from the vendor as to the results from its execution; in GitHub, this is found in the "Actions" tab of the repository (along with the list of automations); see Figure 4-4.

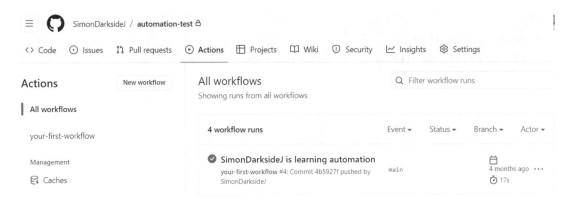

Figure 4-4. *GitHub Actions workflow run*

Opening a completed workflow, whether it was successful or not, will show the full results of that run, as shown in Figure 4-5.

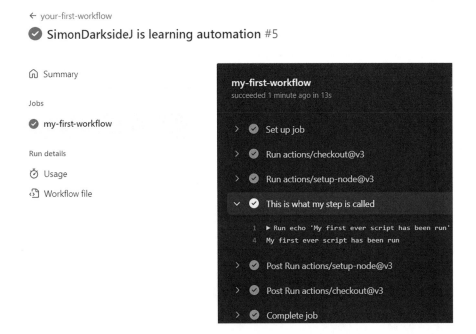

Figure 4-5. *GitHub run output*

As we break this down, we can look at what is happening behind the scenes; as the job "warms up" and prepares an environment to run, we can see everything as it is provisioned, as shown in Figure 4-6.

Figure 4-6. *GitHub run setup step*

From the step to check out the code from the repository, we can see where the code is coming from and, more importantly, where it is going to (especially useful for self-hosted runners on your own server).

Figure 4-7. *GitHub run checkout output*

If you have any prerequisite requirements or dependencies set up, you can also see these enacted, such as the requirement to set up NodeJS in our example workflow, as shown in Figure 4-8.

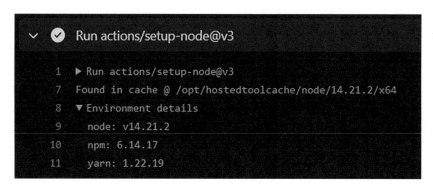

Figure 4-8. *GitHub run setup node output*

Then finally, once the workflow is complete, the environment cleans up after itself, clears out its cache and memory, and prepares for the next big thing, as Figure 4-9 shows.

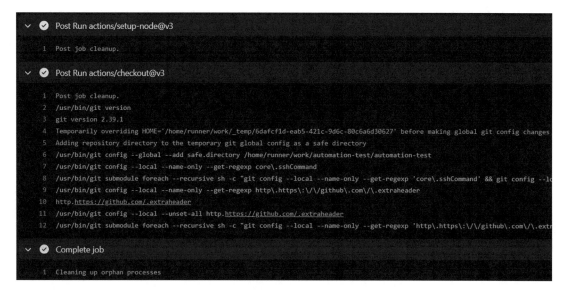

Figure 4-9. *GitHub run post checkout cleanup output*

Most automation platforms give you similar detail, even Unity (although in log form), to help you diagnose issues and validate whether your workflow is operating correctly or not; if not, then you should have sufficient information to make changes to the workflow if needed or diagnose issues with your solution; any errors or exceptions will show up in the log to guide you.

Also of note is that the logs will also show any custom output. You will be writing LOTS of output/echo statements to write to the log manually as you build out your workflows to figure out why your creation isn't doing what you told it to do. **Hint**: It is always your fault, as the automation only does what YOU tell it 😄.

Summary

This chapter is one you will likely keep referring to from time to time or use it as a reference to dive deeper into the docs of the specific service you are trying to implement. Once learned, it is quite easy to adapt and build from as things move forward; the hardest part (as ever) is deciding how far down the rabbit hole you want to go.

As the book unfolds, we will next look at where you want to run your hosting before giving a wider view of the most common and critical tasks that automation is used for.

CHAPTER 5

Automation Hosting

Choosing where your automation is going to run is a critical decision which affects the speed, cost, and availability for your backend processes.

For most providers, there are always options for where to run your automation with various levels of cost that determine how much of the system is maintained by the vendor or whether you endure the operational expenses for the system yourself.

Some of the most common scenarios used are

- Hosting as a service – Agents run on an available agent within the vendor's hosted pool of servers.

- Hosting on a vendor virtual machine – A hosted machine, run and operated by the vendor.

- Hosting via a container run on a Windows or Linux host – Containers are "mini server environments" which are highly scalable. It is also useful if your application "runs" in a container.

- Hosting in a vendor-provided physical machine – All the benefits of a hosted service but at a higher cost to guarantee availability/speed.

© Simon Jackson 2023
S. Jackson, *Accelerating Unity Through Automation*, https://doi.org/10.1007/978-1-4842-9508-3_5

Hosted Runners

For the most part, hosted runners are maintained, operated, and paid for by the vendor, enabling you to purchase or cost for only the time and bandwidth used to run your workflows when they run.

- All operating system updates, packages, tools, and necessary agents are maintained by the vendor.

- The vendor is responsible for all cloud-hosted or physical server costs.

- Ensures a clean workspace for every operation.

- Likely offers a free tier to encourage use with additional costs ramping up in the minutes used.

- May offer dedicated options for specific hardware/cloud availability.

- Normally is operated regionally, where regional latency is required.

- Integration with the vendor's other offerings such as CDN (Content Delivery Networks) and deployment.

Considerations

Table 5-1 lists out some of the considerations you should take into account when using hosted runners.

Table 5-1. *Considerations when using hosted runners*

Consideration	Pros	Cons	Thoughts
Speed	Normally fast based on the type of host requested	In peak demand, it can slow down or take time to run	You can improve access by paying for higher tier access if you need
Concurrency and availability	Normally always available with as many concurrent jobs as your contract allows	Outages are normally widespread across the vendor, unless paying more	Availability is not normally an issue, but you can pay more for more capacity
Cost	Most vendors offer significant free minutes/hours	If you exceed the free access, working out how much you could pay can be sometimes tricky	It all depends on demand; if your load is intensive, you will end up paying sooner, but the free tiers give you a lot of scope for smaller tasks
Availability	Normally guaranteed	Depending on tier/access, you could be in a queue for running jobs	Cloud offers the best availability for the smallest cost, but unless you are in a higher paid tier, you join the global queue

Self-Hosted Runners

The DIY option is very attractive when costs need to be kept to a minimum and where spare hardware can be found at low cost, effectively though, compared to hosted solutions, you are simply retaining the burden for the server's maintenance and operation unto yourself. It can seem daunting, but once it has been set up, personally, I have never had much issue hosting my own.

- You are responsible for keeping the host OS up to date and secure.

- Any additional tools, software not provided by the automation service, need to be maintained and kept up to date.

- You are also responsible for any breaking changes in setup, incompatibility between solutions, or integration.

- If you also host your agent in a cloud virtual machine, obviously you are paying for its hosting too.

- Any hardware failures are yours to deal with, as is redundancy, so ensure you have sufficient spare hardware available in case of failure.

- The cached environment must be maintained by yourself (although personally, if you have large projects, keeping the cache can also be beneficial).

But even with all of the above, you can still use hosted services as a backup in case of failure, providing your automation scripts are built to work in either environment.

Considerations

Table 5-2 lists out some of the considerations you should take into account when using self-hosted runners.

Table 5-2. *Considerations when using self-hosted runners*

Consideration	Pros	Cons	Thoughts
Speed	Reusing hardware you have available	You must maintain the hardware/operating environment	You can use as many machines as you want with as many agents on each, meaning you have more control
Cost	No outlay for existing hardware and easy/cheap to buy/build alternatives	Value is deferred for the company, meaning it also must be managed	Cheapest is not always best, but it is in your control
Concurrency and availability	You can control how much you have depending on criticality	Hardware is not 100% reliable, so you need to plan for spare/backup availability on demand	As any machine is usable as a backup, even developer machines, this can be managed effectively
Availability	Hardware can be anywhere accessible to the Internet on demand, even staff homes	Dependent on hardware being online and backups available	You can scale how you wish, wherever you wish, just be sure to compensate for access

Third-Party Hosting

There are additional vendors that provide customized solutions for hosting, whether they are simply pre-built machines for specific requirements (such as servers preloaded with Unity) or open solutions that you can customize yourself through your automation scripts. In most cases, this is used for very specific situations, such as Mac build hosting, which can be cheaper to run on dedicated Mac server farms.

- Like hosted, the server hardware and operating system updates are maintained by the vendor.

- Additional required software, unless provided in a specific server image, is maintained by you.

- Environment operation and cleanup is usually on request, or some providers offer scheduled jobs to perform cleanup on demand.

- Servers are usually available on demand, so availability is not usually an issue (depending on your vendor package).

Considerations

Table 5-3 lists out some of the considerations you should take into account when using third-party hosted runners.

Table 5-3. *Considerations when using third-party hosted runners*

Consideration	Pros	Cons	Thoughts
Speed	Scalable demand with larger hosts	Costs are exponential and limited per-minute billing	Dedicated virtual machines and constantly available hosts are good for critical situations where demand is high
Cost	Managed costs, normally with fixed prices	Highest running costs	Having always-on hardware will cost more overall
Concurrency and availability	Availability is normally very high, with multiple redundancy	Always comes back to cost overall	Dedicated hosts whether virtual or physical will always be available by contract
Availability	You have your own cloud hardware, which vendors will guarantee	Always on means always charged	The high critical choice

Deciding Factors and Summary

The path you choose will ultimately be your decision; it is just a matter of balancing the cost and effort of maintaining the automation alongside whatever you are building or powering with your configuration.

Simply keep in mind "for each task" (remember, you don't need just one automation, you can have as many as you need):

- What resources are required to operate it?

- How intensive is the task?

- Are there any dependencies that will limit how the automation runs?

- How often does the task need to run: on commit, hourly, daily, weekly, or on demand?

- Are there any localization requirements for pushing/deploying the automation output?

Using these factors and the preceding comparison should help guide you as to where your automation ultimately needs to run.

CHAPTER 6

Validation, Checking Your Code

As a developer, from junior to senior (and beyond), your first duty is to ensure that the code you write meets the needs it is designed for and (almost above all) is clear to understand and, as much as possible, well documented. The task to ensure these guidelines are followed is VERY tedious and often time-consuming for all developers and reviewers involved, whether it is the ping-pong back and forth between the reviewer and the author or different people's opinions about how code is written and managed; this is the time that takes developers away from the fun times of just writing code.

It is far better to agree to the guidelines in advance and have automation set the bar for the standards that must be adhered to for functionality to be accepted into the core product, with exceptions of course.

In this chapter, we will go over some of the available options to support your project, which you can choose to append to your workflows and practices.

As these automations all pertain to operations on your source code, they are only targeted for Azure Pipelines and GitHub Actions; Unity Gaming Services has no such concept – although you can still implement them in your source code repositories.

© Simon Jackson 2023
S. Jackson, *Accelerating Unity Through Automation*, https://doi.org/10.1007/978-1-4842-9508-3_6

Before We Start

A quick note before we dive in, you will see that most workflows require a "token" to operate; this is simply a Personal Access Token (PAT) that has the rights to perform the activities on your repository:

```
token: "${{ secrets.GITHUB_TOKEN }}"
```

Just make sure you have generated a PAT using either your automation user (or your own account, although this is not advised) and you have registered it within the Secrets area for your Azure Pipelines or GitHub Actions.

Check Chapter 4 for more details about registering secrets and variables.

Welcome Greetings

SUITABLE FOR	GITHUB ACTIONS

If you are running an open source project, it is always good to be nice and welcoming to any visitor that decides to get involved, raise issues, or even submit a PR request with some much-needed fixes; to this end, GitHub provides an out-of-the-box solution to help with just that.

The First Interaction GitHub Actions identifies when a user has their first interaction for issues or pull requests and then sends them a greeting of your choosing, as in Figure 6-1.

- https://github.com/actions/first-interaction

```
name: Greetings

on: [pull_request_target, issues]

jobs:
  greeting:
    runs-on: ubuntu-latest
    permissions:
      issues: write
      pull-requests: write
    steps:
    - uses: actions/first-interaction@v1
      with:
        repo-token: ${{ secrets.GITHUB_TOKEN }}
        issue-message: "Message that will be displayed on users' first issue"
        pr-message: "Message that will be displayed on users' first pull request"
```

Figure 6-1. *First Interaction sample automation YAML*

Setting Labels

SUITABLE FOR	**GITHUB ACTIONS**

With larger teams (and some cases, smaller projects with lots of components), categorization is key, having a quick and identifiable way of knowing what feature or component a **PR** is targeting specifically, which goes a long way to maximize efficiency, just by simply preventing developers from having to trawl through a massive list of items and focus only on those things they are responsible for.

This is where GitHub's Labeler Action comes in very useful, as it allows you to predetermine what labels are associated with PRs at the time of creation and, if you desire, even keep those labels up to date as work continues.

- https://github.com/actions/labeler

Configuring the YAML workflow needed for this automation is very small (Figure 6-2).

```
name: Labeler
on: [pull_request_target]

jobs:
  label:

    runs-on: ubuntu-latest
    permissions:
      contents: read
      pull-requests: write

    steps:
    - uses: actions/labeler@v4
      with:
        repo-token: "${{ secrets.GITHUB_TOKEN }}"
```

Figure 6-2. *Labeler sample automation YAML*

Additionally, however, you will also need a "**labeler.yml**" file in your "**.github**" folder to give the Labeler action enough information to do the categorization, for which the format of this file is very simple:

```
# Add the 'my-feature' label to any PRs that change any files in the
'features/myawesomefeature' folder or any subfolders.
my-feature:
- features/myawesomefeature/**/*

# Add the 'docs' label to any PRs that change any of the documentation
files in the repository.
docs:
- *.md
```

Ensuring Assignment

SUITABLE FOR	**GITHUB ACTIONS**

When PRs are created, the responsible thing to do is to ensure that the person ultimately responsible for that PR is assigned to it; I've lost count of the times PRs "turn up" in a repository, and only the list of contributors of a PR gives you any indication who has been working on it, which is sometimes a lot of people to chase down to ask questions to. A simple way to avoid this is to add a check to ensure the "Assignees" property for a PR is populated before the PR can go anywhere.

Thankfully, the community has provided the option here with the Assign PR Creator Action, and it is a quick and easy GitHub Actions to add to any repository, as shown in Figure 6-3.

- https://github.com/thomaseizinger/assign-pr-creator-action

```yaml
name: Assign PR to creator

on: [pull_request]

jobs:
  automation:
    runs-on: ubuntu-latest
    steps:
    - name: Assign PR to creator
      uses: thomaseizinger/assign-pr-creator-action@v1.0.0
      # Optionally add an IF clause to only check when the PR is first opened.
      if: github.event_name == 'pull_request' && github.event.action ==
'opened'
      with:
        repo-token: ${{ secrets.GITHUB_TOKEN }}
```

Figure 6-3. *Assign PR Creator sample automation YAML*

The action is quite old now but still very good as not that much has changed in the GitHub API for some time.

Formatting PR Titles

SUITABLE FOR	**GITHUB ACTIONS**

On public source repositories where you are likely to get multiple PR requests from external contributors, it can be very handy to define a structure for how a PR is titled, so that it clearly states what the PR is intended to do, what it is doing it to, and a clear description, just from its title. The recommended standard for this is the Conventional Commits specification (`www.conventionalcommits.org/`), which outlines the following pattern:

feat(ui): Add Button component

- *feat = Subject, feature*

- *(ui) = Scope, the specific feature being updated*

- *Add = Type, what type of change is this*

It is a very specific requirement to demand this on PRs but is very useful to make things clear to maintainers on what PRs are doing and saves a lot of time (as well as making the contributor think about what they are adding).

- `https://github.com/amannn/action-semantic-pull-request`

The YAML to enable this is shown in Figure 6-4.

```
name: "PR Convention"

on:
  pull_request_target:
    types:
      - opened
      - edited
      - synchronize

jobs:
  main:
    name: Validate PR title
    runs-on: ubuntu-latest
    steps:
      - uses: amannn/action-semantic-pull-request@v5
        env:
          GITHUB_TOKEN: ${{ secrets.GITHUB_TOKEN }}
```

Figure 6-4. *Semantic pull request sample automation YAML*

This ensures that on any PR when it is first opened or edited, the convention is followed. There are also many additional options available on the GitHub Actions Marketplace for this action, which you should review when looking to implement this option.

- https://github.com/marketplace/actions/semantic-pull-request

Code Scanning

SUITABLE FOR	GITHUB ACTIONS

There has been a lot of focus of late regarding the wellness and secure state for any code written today, mainly to ensure the pitfalls of the past are not replicated but also to ensure future use is written in a safe and secure manner; to this end, GitHub already performs basic scanning tests on all repositories and, where possible, dependencies of those repositories to ensure the administrators of those repositories are informed and can take appropriate action as required.

You can read about GitHub's code scanning efforts here:

- `https://docs.github.com/en/code-security/code-scanning/`
  `automatically-scanning-your-code-for-vulnerabilities-and-`
  `errors/about-code-scanning`

  In addition to GitHub's default operations, there are many samples for adding language-specific Actions for your codebase, far too many to list here due to the sheer number of languages.

  You can see the list of example code scanning automations here, with each language in a separate YAML file that you can copy and add to your GitHub automation library in your repository:

- `https://github.com/actions/starter-workflows/tree/main/`
  `code-scanning`

Documentation

SUITABLE FOR	GITHUB ACTIONS

To close this chapter, we will investigate automatic documentation generation using GitHub Actions, which can come in two forms:

- Generate documentation from static sources like Jekyll, Docusaurus, and Microsoft PSDocs.

- Generate dynamic documentation from code documentation using services like DocFX.

Static Documentation

I have worked with so many different solutions for managing a project's documentation over the years; they all kind of blend in together, but ultimately the goal is the same:

- Ensure you keep the source of the documentation clean so that developers do not need to worry about formatting and can just write about the code.

- Use build routines to validate that the written documentation works (no broken links, etc.).

- Apply standards-based formatting to the output for the hosting.

Static documentation usually requires a separate repository, although many I talk to prefer to keep the code documentation available in the same repository as the code to keep things aligned; there is no right or wrong way to manage this in reality.

- Microsoft's PSDocs format writes documentation using code, which can align closely to the code that is written.

  You can read about PSDocs at `https://github.com/microsoft/PSDocs` and its corresponding GitHub Actions for generating the documentation at `https://github.com/microsoft/ps-docs`.

- Whereas Docusaurus generates a Markdown-friendly way of writing documentation which is then converted into HTML for static viewing using a GitHub Actions (which I personally prefer)

  You can read more about Docusaurus at `https://github.com/facebook/docusaurus`; just be sure to also check out their guide for publishing to GitHub pages at (GitHub's free web hosting) `https://docusaurus.io/docs/deployment#deploying-to-github-pages`.

Dynamic Documentation Generation

The most favored tool for API or Dynamic document generation is a tool from Microsoft called **DocFX** (there are others, but most use DocFX); DocFX reads the code API looking for "Summary" and "Properties" documentation tags (as shown in Figure 6-5) and then generates an API website based on the selected theme.

```
/// <summary>
/// Data type that represents a vector3.
/// </summary>
public struct UnitVector3 : IEquatable<UnitVector3>
{
    /// <summary>
    /// Initializes a new instance of the <see cref="UnitVector3"/>
struct.
    /// </summary>
    /// <param name="x">The x value.</param>
    /// <param name="y">The y value.</param>
    /// <param name="z">The z value.</param>
    public UnitVector3(float x, float y, float z)
    {
        this.X = x;
        this.Y = y;
        this.Z = z;
    }

    /// <summary>
    /// Gets a vector whose 3 elements are equal to zero.
    /// </summary>
    /// <returns>
    /// A vector whose three elements are equal to zero (that is, it
returns the vector (0,0,0) ).
    /// </returns>
    public static UnitVector3 Zero
    {
        get
        {
            return default;
        }
    }
}
```

Figure 6-5. *Code with "Summary" tags example*

This is used by most vendor solutions out there for maintaining their documentation, from Microsoft, Unity, and more.

Getting DocFX to run through automation is fairly easy these days and is clearly documented on the DocFX website here: `https://dotnet.github.io/docfx/`. Once you have configured a "**docfx.json**" configuration file, you will then need to add the automation to your repository to generate it (Figure 6-6).

See the DocFX documentation at `https://dotnet.github.io/docfx/docs/config.html` for more details on how to customize DocFX for your project.

```yaml
name: Build API docs

on:
  workflow_dispatch:

concurrency:
  group: ${{ github.ref }}
  cancel-in-progress: true

jobs:
  publish-docs:
    runs-on: ubuntu-latest
    steps:
    - name: Checkout
      uses: actions/checkout@v3
    - name: Dotnet Setup
      uses: actions/setup-dotnet@v3
      with:
        dotnet-version: 7.x

    - run: dotnet tool update -g docfx
    - run: docfx docfx_project/docfx.json

    - name: Deploy
      uses: peaceiris/actions-gh-pages@v3
      with:
        github_token: ${{ secrets.GITHUB_TOKEN }}
        publish_dir: docs/_site
```

Figure 6-6. *DocFX deployment automation example*

When run, it will perform the following operations:

- Check out the latest copy of your repository.

- Look for the "**docfx.json**" configuration file in "**docfx_project/docfx. json**" (update this if you have it elsewhere).

- Finally, thanks to a community GitHub Actions, it will create/update a branch called "**gh-pages**" by default (which you will need to configure in your Project Settings) with the generated content.

Note   The compiled pages are not put back into your base repository, they are generated fresh each time.

The result will be something like what you see in Figure 6-7 (an example from the DocFX website).

API / Microsoft.DocAsCode

Class BuildOptions

Namespace: Microsoft.DocAsCode
Assembly: Microsoft.DocAsCode.App.dll

Provides options to be used with Build(string, BuildOptions).

```
public class BuildOptions
```

Inheritance
object ← BuildOptions

Inherited Members
object.Equals(object) , object.Equals(object, object) , object.GetHashCode() , object.GetType() , object.MemberwiseClone() ,
object.ReferenceEquals(object, object) , object.ToString()

Properties

ConfigureMarkdig

Configures the markdig markdown pipeline.

```
public Func<MarkdownPipelineBuilder, MarkdownPipelineBuilder>? ConfigureMarkdig { get; init; }
```

Property Value

Func <MarkdownPipelineBuilder, MarkdownPipelineBuilder>

Figure 6-7. *DocFX example output*

Summary

This chapter gives you a glimpse into the world of managing the repository itself which should work on most platforms that support automation through the source control platform. Granted, we have focused solely on GitHub Actions for this chapter, mainly because of everything GitHub has to offer in this area, and it is also as close to your source as you can get.

This is just a taste, and I recommend you look at each repository you work with, from Microsoft to GitHub's own repositories, and learn from them any additional validation tasks that you might find useful for maintaining your codebase.

Next, let us move on to the world of testing, a fraught and dark place where many fear to tread.

## CHAPTER 7

Testing, Making Sure It Runs

When your code is checked in, the last thing you want is to find out hours, days, or months later that some change had an unintended effect that will cause you mountains of headaches as you are struggling to release; there are ways to counter these, but all will add additional effort to your production line; there is no such thing as a free lunch.

However, using automation, the time spent building a workflow is not wasted and can prevent the worst kinds of issues which will ultimately cost you more in the long run.

The obvious issues to find are always the easiest to fix; it is the unintentional bug that only happens when you finally run in a certain way or on a particular platform which will cause you the most grief and time.

The protections implemented using automation WILL save you time (and therefore money) in the long run, despite the steep learning curve and time required to perfect a workflow, which can range from (simplest to intensive)

1. Running a build and making sure it compiles

2. Running the same build multiple times over several platforms

3. Executing the solution on a platform (different from a build)

4. Creating unit tests to validate code does what it says it does and catching variations

© Simon Jackson 2023
S. Jackson, *Accelerating Unity Through Automation*, https://doi.org/10.1007/978-1-4842-9508-3_7

The "rule of thumb" is to apply these in order and gauge their effectiveness, although personally 2 and 4 are my go-to, which I try and apply where it fits, or more rather to say, "I always implement No. 1, and where possible, I apply No. 4, but not always and not on everything."

Where automation comes into play is that automation can save countless hours running multiple builds and tests in the background so that you only need to check the results or use them as safeguards against anything unwarranted getting into your project. It is all "automated" 😊.

Doing Builds

We all build our Unity project eventually, as it is the only way to get your solution onto a device and run it (else, what is the point), but how frequently we do this can be very indeterminate; in a lot of firms I have consulted with, a build is only done when a checkpoint is met or when the client needs to see something running. This can be VERY bad, as it relies on all developers in a team checking their code constantly, but no one is checking it all fits together until the end.

The reason for this behavior is simple: making builds takes time, and in most cases a LOT of time, which most developers can seldom afford because it stops them developing. Simply relying on the Unity console is simply not enough though, as there are so many factors to consider when Unity crunches the numbers and compiles all your code to produce a build for a single platform.

In most cases, simply doing the Unity build itself through automation is enough, just making sure that Unity outputs "something"; the output does not need to be run, just the fact that Unity "can" build for a specific platform is enough to catch 80% of the common issues encountered when building Unity projects. However, remember, just because Unity can build for a single platform does not mean it will build for all platforms, mainly due to the complex nature of certain platforms and code/API incompatibilities that can occur.

Per Commit/PR Testing

A simple solution is to validate the code every time it is checked in and "pushed" to the server, letting other machines do the builds in the background and have safeguards to ensure that developers cannot push code that will break the build, using automation as the safeguard for your sanity. If the build fails, it can add time to the developer's day to find the issue and fix it, but you are fixing early while the code is fresh in the developer's mind.

Granted, developers need to remember to push their code regularly, either per fix or daily, in order for the automation to do its work; if it is not on the server, there is nothing that can be done, and in the worse cases, if something should happen to the developer's workstation before the updates are committed and pushed, the work will be lost.

Nightly Builds

Another approach, usually used in conjunction with the commit testing, is to perform nightly or weekly builds of all the work completed to that date; this is usually more intensive as it is a one-off task; however, the results of such a test need to be managed to ensure the right people are informed if issues are found.

Nightly builds are usually distributed to Quality teams, who will run/play the project to ensure specific goals have been met and no obvious issues have crept in.

Solutions

Chapters 9–11 will cover all the requirements for performing builds and the tools used in their operation, ranging from

- Unity Gaming Services (UGS) DevOps – With the sole task of creating a build

- Unity DevOps Extension for Azure Pipelines – Which is very fast and can be streamlined for multiple builds on Azure Pipelines

- GameCI Actions for GitHub Actions – Hosted building of Unity projects with very clean environments

- Custom scripting – Available for either Azure Pipelines or GitHub Actions, although you can inject additional operations with UGS through Unity scripting

In addition to these, your source control provider can be configured to ensure it only lets code be merged once all the checks have passed, often referred to as "**Branch Protections**," as shown in Figure 7-1.

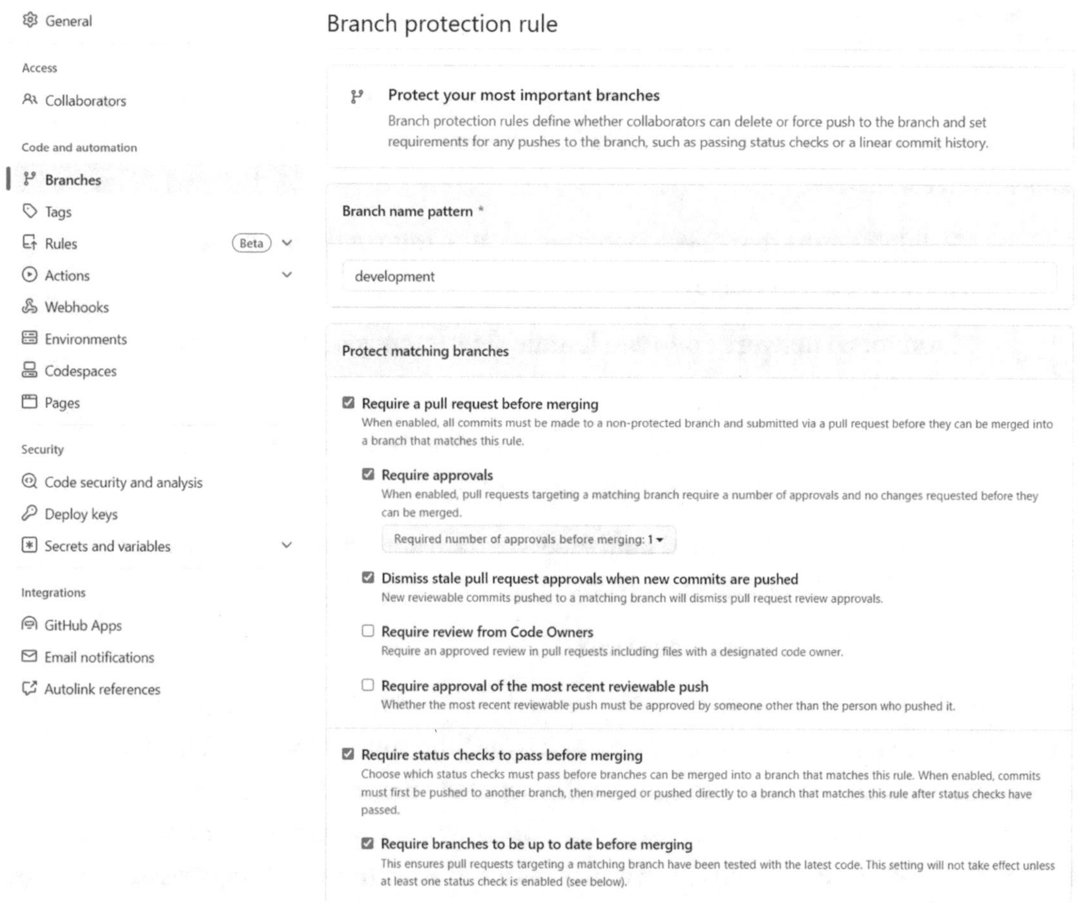

Figure 7-1. *GitHub Branch Protections*

For each named branch (you can have different rules for different branches), you can specify the conditions that **MUST** be met for code to be accepted into that branch. With the automations defined, whether it is Azure Pipelines or GitHub Actions, failures are blocked until they are resolved. This can be overridden by administrators when needed, but for the most part, it safeguards the repository against faulty code/builds being entered.

Additionally, it is also recommended that you check all the platforms you intend to target; this will incur a longer time for validations to take place but will save you time later. However, only if you do intend to deploy to that platform, do not just do it to make sure it will work in the future.

Unit Testing

Often seen as the bane for any developer, unit testing can be almost just as crucial as doing build testing as it can identify subtle changes that result in unintended consequences, such as

- Validates code that checks whether a value returned from code is within a certain range

- Monitors if network code can handle slow latency or if it causes race conditions

- Identifies that a set of options is what is expected, and no additional options have been added (without checks)

- Ensures that transmitted data meets certain specifications and can be serialized/deserialized correctly

- Dreaded NULL reference errors

While all these sound awesome, they incur a high cost to implement, as in every case for what you are testing, you are trying to "catch out" the code being tested to ensure it works, which requires even more code written around other code to do the checks and balances; often seen as the main reason developers either shy away from or prefer not to write testing code is that it is NOT fun and takes them away from building awesome things.

Personally, I like to add safeguards around critical functions so that they can be validated prior to builds; it also protects my code from unintentional changes from other developers who try and add new features only to find out later it broke my magical functions. If done right, they can be quick and easy to write, but if done as an afterthought or later, they can quickly become a real headache.

Unit tests are effectively a separate project from the main code, and Unity provides two flavors of testing to implement, namely:

- Editor run tests – Generally code-checking tests that are run in the background without a project running

- Play mode tests – For testing code/scenes when they are running to ensure they behave correctly

---

You can read more about the Unity Testing Framework here:

`https://docs.unity3d.com/Packages/com.unity.test-framework@1.3/manual/index.html`

Unity even added full tests to their Lost Crypt sample to demonstrate the use of the testing framework.

An Example

Unit tests are hard to demonstrate as it requires you to understand the code you are writing and what you should expect as the output and knowing what values are unacceptable, for example, if we take the following class which simply adds two numbers together, we should know what to expect:

```
public class MyClass
{
    public int Add(int a, int b)
    {
        return a + b;
    }
}
```

In testing this, we can define a Testing class to validate how this function operates and give it some test values to check:

```
public class MyClassTests
{
    [Test]
    [TestCase(24, 80, 104)]
    [TestCase(10, -15, -5)]
    [TestCase(int.MaxValue, 10, int.MinValue + 9)]
    public void AddCalculatesCorrectValue(int valueA, int valueB, int
    expectedResult)
    {
        var myClass = new MyClass();

        var result = myClass.Add(valueA, valueB);

        Assert.That(result, Is.EqualTo(expectedResult));
    }
}
```

Here, we

- Create a new instance of "MyClass".

- Add the two inputs together and capture the output.

- Check the output is the value we are testing for in the "expected result" using "Assert.That".

- Provide three "test cases" where we submit those values to be tested.

When run through the "Unity Test Runner" (which can be found under "*Window* ➤ *General* ➤ *Test Runner*"), we would get the output shown in Figure 7-2.

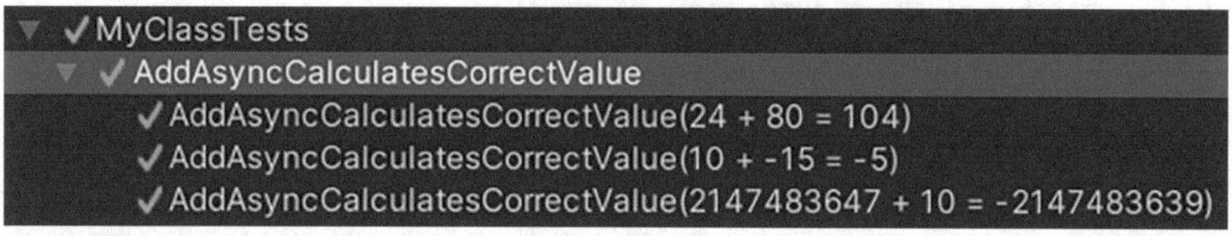

Figure 7-2. Unity Test Runner output

This is a very simple test to be sure, and there are many more examples in the Test Framework package and the Lost Crypt demo, but where this becomes crucial is when the code being run is CRITICAL to the operation of your project, and any changes in output or the handling of an input can cause severe issues in your project like

- If the "MyClass" Add function used strings as input and someone tried to send it Unicode characters, it would produce weird results.

- If the "MyClass" Add function had objects as input and a new feature forgot to assign a value to one of them, it would crash. (Granted, it should have null reference handling in the function, but the unit test would identify this earlier.)

- If your UI used the output of a function to load a specific image from the project, but the image did not exist, it would cause graphical issues. (Typos are REAL!)

- If your code called out to a network endpoint but could not handle it when there was no network.

Granted, most of these could be handled if the developer tested the code they wrote when they wrote it, but that is not always the case, and it could just as easily be another developer consuming a function and "expecting" it to work in a way it was not designed for, or even an artist adds a new UI and updates a config file to add that UI, but the code cannot recognize it.

There are many reasons unit testing can be critical to the safeguarding of your project, but always at the cost of time and thought in its implementation, but a lifesaver for when the unthinkable happens. It is important to ensure that testing validates both the "correct" operation for a function, but also to check if the "wrong thing" is used as an input and, even more critically, check when things could be NULL (null reference errors are the hardest to track down in a running project).

Running Unit Tests

Alongside the Unity Test Framework, the Unity editor has a "Test" mode that it can be run in, which most Pipeline Extensions and GitHub actions recognize; this allows a "special" build of Unity (assuming Unity can build it) to then go on and run the unit tests on the compiled code. This is not a full build, and no build output is generated, but it allows Unity to run all your tests and report back on them.

Granted, the XML that is generated in the output can be VERY hard to read, so in most cases the unit tests fail, you get an indication of which tests have failed, and then you can build/test the project locally to find the cause.

I cannot overstate the number of times, especially on VERY large projects, where unit tests have prevented critical issues from being introduced into a live project, and it goes to show that just because a project CAN be built does NOT mean it should be given to customers!

Summary

This has been a fairly wordy chapter to highlight two of the main critical steps that are often the first things that automation can take over, running builds and running tests, both of which can identify critical problems far sooner and more cheaply than having multiple developers pouring over code and ripping things apart to figure out why one of the player screens suddenly has lost all its graphics and causes the project to crash when opened (never happened of course, because I was testing, honest).

In the next chapter, we will continue this path to finally getting a build out and handling the myriad of trials that can bring.

CHAPTER 8

Building and Publishing

As we reach the end of all the background of automation and before we show how to put it together for the three services covered in this chapter, we head into troubled waters regarding automating Unity builds, actually making builds.

It might sound like the simplest of tasks, but as ever, the last 10% always causes at least 80% of the effort, and building in Unity is no different. This is mainly due to the following factors:

- Some platforms require an additional build step which Unity itself does not cover (once Unity has done its thing, it is done with it).

- Unity switched its build processes to build scripting but didn't really tell anyone. That and the old build process is still there and "mostly" works, until it doesn't.

- Specific elements of Unity's asset pipeline are platform dependent (such as addressables), and issues do not start to surface until either the build or later once things are deployed.

There are more, and you will no doubt run into them as you try and automate your builds, which might lead you to think "why bother," but after your umpteenth build and reaching the end of your bottomless cup of coffee, you will remember why, watching the Unity progress bar is not good for your mental health.

Forewarning This is one of the more involved chapters of this title, as Unity does not always make this easy. Best to strap in for a long rough ride and wear your most comfortable riding trousers.

© Simon Jackson 2023
S. Jackson, *Accelerating Unity Through Automation*, https://doi.org/10.1007/978-1-4842-9508-3_8

Here is what we will cover:

- Building and concurrency

- Unity Build scripting, including addressables

- Building UPM packages

- Building additional platforms, Windows, iOS

- Pushing out a release

Build Concurrency

Two critical things to consider for any pipeline, but even more critical for builds is concurrency, that being:

- If a build is running and I submit a change, does it cancel the previous build?

- Can I build more than one platform at once (provided I have the hardware)?

Both are essential when considering automation, even if you are only building for a single platform now; if you are considering adding other platforms later, include them with the pipeline anyway, just to ensure you do not introduce changes that are either irrevocable or will cause major rewrites and headaches later. Never put off until tomorrow what your automation can test today ☺.

Workflow Concurrency

⊙ SUITABLE FOR	**GITHUB ACTIONS**

Managing wherever builds can cancel each other out is something you have to enable; by default, a build will run and run until it is finished, no matter how many you have lined up. Thankfully, this is very easy to override with a simple definition added to your workflow, as in Figure 8-1.

```
concurrency:
  group: ${{ github.workflow }}-${{ github.ref }}
  cancel-in-progress: true
```

Figure 8-1. *GitHub Actions workflow concurrency*

This defines

- The main concurrency capability in GitHub Actions

- The group or mechanism to group builds

- Additional flag to enable "cancel-in-progress"

With these three elements, any build for the same target (branch/repository) will cancel the currently running action straightaway (no waiting for Unity to think about whether it wants to cancel or wait until it is not busy). This saves time and money from builds known to fail or that last minute "oh I forgot to change this" moments, so you do not need to wait until the last build was finished to wait for the results.

Changes to other branches will not be affected, so if multiple developers have builds running, it will only affect the workflow being built for the branch you are changing.

You can change the behavior if you wish to cancel any build that is running when a new build is requested by simply altering the scope of the "**group**" to what is shown in Figure 8-2.

```
concurrency:
  group: ${{ github.ref }}
  cancel-in-progress: true
```

Figure 8-2. *GitHub Actions concurrency behavior to cancel all jobs*

Sadly, UGS does not have this capability (at the time of writing), and while Azure Pipelines can, however, it is cost prohibitive as you need to upgrade to a more expensive license to enable concurrent builds.

Parallel Builds

The other concurrency behavior we can apply in automation is the ability to set up what is called a "strategy" whereby you define a matrix of parameters, such as build platform, arguments, and overrides, and then use these to run the same workflow multiple times using those arguments.

These are defined in YAML using the pattern shown in Table 8-1.

Table 8-1. *Matrix strategy definitions for GitHub Actions and Azure Pipelines*

Azure Pipelines	GitHub Actions

strategy:
 matrix:
  buildAndroid:
   os: self-hosted-windows
   build-target: Android
 	
  buildWindows:
   os: self-hosted-windows
   build-target: StandaloneWindows64
 	
  buildWindows:
   os: self-hosted-mac
   build-target: iOS
	strategy:
	 matrix:
	 include:
	  - os: self-hosted-windows
	   build-target: Android
	  - os: self-hosted-windows
	   build-target: Standalone
	   Windows64
	  - os: self-hosted-mac
	   build-target: iOS

As you can see, the format of each is very similar with only subtle differences, both describing the following:

- Strategy – Declare a strategy component.

- Matrix – Declare a new matrix array of work.

- Array – The declarative array of settings that can be referenced.

There are many ways to configure a matrix, each resulting in larger and more complex arrangements of jobs, up to a maximum of 256 running at any given time.

Check the respective documentation for each vendor for additional data in ways you can configure Matrices:

Azure Pipelines: `https://learn.microsoft.com/en-us/azure/devops/ pipelines/get-started-multiplatform?view=azure-devops`

GitHub Actions: `https://docs.github.com/en/actions/using-jobs/ using-a-matrix-for-your-jobs`

For Unity solutions, the simpler the better when configuring your Matrices, as if you get too complex, you could lead to some "very" odd combinations, only made worse that certain builds are only supported on certain platforms (e.g., iOS on MacOS).

With a matrix defined, utilizing it is very easy as we simply use the following pattern to retrieve the current matrix value for the current run for either Azure or GitHub:

```
## Azure Pipelines
$(os)
```

```
## GitHub Actions
 ${{ matrix.os }}
```

For GitHub, we specify "Matrix" being the fact we are calling on the Matrix and the "variable name" we custom-defined that is being used in this run; for Azure, we can simply call on the "variable name" as it is declared globally for each run (although I prefer the way GitHub Actions does it). The preceding matrix results in THREE runs:

- One for building Android on our self-hosted-windows agent

- Another run for StandaloneWindows64, also on our self-hosted-windows agent

- And finally, one for building iOS on a self-hosted-mac agent

All three will run in parallel (saving lots of time), and if any single one fails, all builds will either cancel or fail (all or nothing); we can override this behavior if you wish, as well as controlling how many concurrent jobs can run at a time (so as not to overload your hosts); for each of these, please review the links provided earlier.

Borrowing a pre-built automation script from Chapter 10, we can demonstrate the use of a Matrix to purposely build a Unity project for multiple platforms; this is only an example to use for reference for now.

Listing 8-1. Sample build YAML with Matrix use

```
trigger:
- main

strategy:
  matrix:
    buildAndroid:
      os: self-hosted-windows
      build-target: Android

    buildWindows:
      os: self-hosted-windows
      build-target: StandaloneWindows64

pool:
  vmImage: $(os)

steps:

- task: UnityGetProjectVersionTask@1
  name: unitygetprojectversion
  inputs:
    unityProjectPath: 'TheMostAwesomeGameEverMade/'

- task: UnitySetupTask@1
  inputs:
    versionSelectionMode: 'specify'
    version: '$(unitygetprojectversion.projectVersion)'
    revision: '$(unitygetprojectversion.projectVersionRevision)'
    installWindowsIL2CPPModule: true
```

```
- task: UnityBuildTask@3
  inputs:
    buildTarget: $(build-target)
    unityProjectPath: 'TheMostAwesomeGameEverMade/'
    versionSelectionMode: 'project'
    outputPath: '$(Build.BinariesDirectory)'
    outputFileName: 'TheMostAwesomeGameEverMade'
```

Please refer to Chapter 10 to understand the full scope of this example.

Using the new Matrix we defined, we use the "**OS**" variable to determine the pool (hosts) the workflow runs on and tell the "Build Task" which Unity platform to build for using the "**Build-Target**" parameter and off it runs.

I recommend looking around other projects on GitHub that are using Azure Pipelines or GitHub actions to look at other variations, as what is described here is only one way (although my preferred way). If you want to see an over-the-top example, check out the reusable pipeline I created for the Reality Collective here:

https://github.com/realitycollective/reusableworkflows/blob/ main/.github/workflows/rununityUPMbuildmultiversion.yml

This script builds for three platforms on three different versions of Unity to validate that a UPM package has no issues with whatever Unity throws at it. It could be shortened, but I have always felt this is clearer.

And in case you have not guessed it, Unity Gaming Services DevOps does not have this level of scripting control, but you can configure multiple platforms and control how they execute through the UI; *check Chapter 9 for more information.*

Unity Build Scripting

Now, in most cases, the extensions, plugins, and options you use will take care of most of the common build tasks for you, managing what you build and where you build it; Unity from the command line will allow you to do "some" things straight out of the box; however, problems occur once you start to run into some edge cases, such as

- Needing a custom Gradle version for Android builds.

- You want to build addressables at build time (actually, UGS does have an option for this).

- Pre- and post-build tasks you need to enact in your build.

- Some custom Asset handling.

- Coffee, more coffee, there is always a need for more coffee or other hot beverages.

The list goes on, but in short, anything outside of just building for basic Android or Windows Standalone will only result in errors or an incomplete build. The reason for this is that since the late Unity 2018 days (Unity 2018.2 to be exact), Unity switched its built-in build pipeline for a Scriptable Build pipeline and seemed to stop maintaining the old version from then on.

You can read the full and detailed Unity Scriptable Build Pipeline documentation here for reference:

`https://docs.unity3d.com/Packages/com.unity.`
`scriptablebuildpipeline@1.21/manual/index.html`

Fair warning The preceding site mostly only talks about just building asset bundles; for more details on all the options for using the BuildPipeline, see the following Unity API guide (another fair warning, it is a bit dry):

`https://docs.unity3d.com/ScriptReference/BuildPipeline.html`

In essence (and what most of the leading packages do), you need to have a special editor build script in your project designed to perform the necessary tasks needed. Finding a good start or an example script is not the easiest thing in the world, but here is what I use by default.

Listing 8-2. Example Scriptable Build script

```
using System;
using System.Collections.Generic;
using System.IO;
using UnityEditor;
using UnityEditor.Build.Reporting;
using UnityEngine;

public static class Builder
{
    public static void BuildProject()
    {
        try
        {
            List<string> ActiveScenePaths = new();
            foreach (EditorBuildSettingsScene scene in EditorBuild
            Settings.scenes)
            {
                if (scene.enabled)
                {
                    ActiveScenePaths.Add(scene.path);
                }
            }
            BuildReport buildReport = default;

            var options = new BuildPlayerOptions
            {
                scenes = ActiveScenePaths.ToArray(),
                target = EditorUserBuildSettings.activeBuildTarget,
                locationPathName = Path.Combine($"build/
                {EditorUserBuildSettings.activeBuildTarget}",
                GetBuildTargetOutputFileNameAndExtension()),
                targetGroup = EditorUserBuildSettings.selectedBuild
                TargetGroup
            };
```

```
            buildReport = BuildPipeline.BuildPlayer(options);

            switch (buildReport.summary.result)
            {
                case BuildResult.Succeeded:
                    EditorApplication.Exit(0);
                    break;
                case BuildResult.Unknown:
                case BuildResult.Failed:
                case BuildResult.Cancelled:
                default:
                    EditorApplication.Exit(1);
                    break;
            }
        }
        catch (Exception ex)
        {
            Debug.Log("BUILD FAILED: " + ex.Message);
            EditorApplication.Exit(1);
        }
    }

    private static string GetBuildTargetOutputFileNameAndExtension()
    {
        switch (EditorUserBuildSettings.activeBuildTarget)
        {
            case BuildTarget.Android:
                return string.Format("{0}.apk", Application.productName);
            case BuildTarget.StandaloneWindows64:
            case BuildTarget.StandaloneWindows:
                return string.Format("{0}.exe", Application.productName);
#if UNITY_2018_1_OR_NEWER
            case BuildTarget.StandaloneOSX:
#endif
#if !UNITY_2017_3_OR_NEWER
                case BuildTarget.StandaloneOSXIntel:
                case BuildTarget.StandaloneOSXIntel64:
```

```
#endif
                return string.Format("{0}.app", Application.productName);
            case BuildTarget.iOS:
            case BuildTarget.tvOS:
            case BuildTarget.WebGL:
            case BuildTarget.WSAPlayer:
            case BuildTarget.StandaloneLinux64:
#if !UNITY_2018_3_OR_NEWER
                case BuildTarget.PSP2:
#endif
            case BuildTarget.PS4:
            case BuildTarget.XboxOne:
#if !UNITY_2017_3_OR_NEWER
                case BuildTarget.SamsungTV:
#endif
#if !UNITY_2018_1_OR_NEWER
                case BuildTarget.N3DS:
                case BuildTarget.WiiU:
#endif
            case BuildTarget.Switch:
            case BuildTarget.NoTarget:
            default:
                return Application.productName;
        }
    }
}
```

There is a lot packed into this script, most of which you never need to worry about, but here is a rundown:

- There is a static class called "**Builder**"; this has to be static as the pipeline will be accessing this script from Unity without the project running.

- A static "**BuildProject**" method is defined that is called by the automation.

- The script starts by getting a list of the scenes configured in the Unity Build Player window, and if the scene is enabled (ticked), it is added to the list of scenes to build (fully customizable of course).

- We create a new "**BuildReport**"; this is essential as without it a Unity build WILL NOT RUN; it is used by Unity to capture what happens in a build.

- We then define the "**BuildPlayerOptions**" used to process the build, including the scene list, build target, where to build it, etc. More options can be added if you wish.

Full BuildPlayerOptions can be found here:

https://docs.unity3d.com/ScriptReference/BuildPlayerOptions.html.

- With the options compiled, you can now run the "**BuildPipeline. BuildPlayer**" using the options we have defined.

Critical You MUST assign the result of the BuildPipeline.BuildPlayer to a BuildReport variable; without it, the build WILL NOT RUN.

buildReport = BuildPipeline.BuildPlayer(options);

The rest of the script (mainly the "**GetBuildTargetOutputFileNameAndExtension**" method) is just about setting the folder and output extension the build should generate, as well as checking the results of the "**BuildReport**" to see if the build was successful or not.

This covers a basic build script, which you might want to customize if you have specific needs or alterations for your build (see the "Addressables" section).

To finish this build script part, you must understand how this script is used by Unity in a build because by default it will be ignored. When you manually run the build, either from the command line or through automation, you MUST update the command with the following:

```
-executeMethod Builder.BuildProject
```

This simply informs the editor to use your custom-built build script instead of its default built-in build process. The full command would be something like this:

```
Unity.exe -projectPath <unityProjectPath> -logfile <logFilePath>
-batchmode -nographics -quit -executeMethod Builder.BuildProject
-outputPath <buildOutputPath> -buildTarget <yourBuildTarget>
```

The options are fairly self-explanatory, obviously replacing the elements surrounded with "<>" with your local versions.

Further Extending the Build Script

A question I often get asked is HOW to pass additional commands to the build script, in case (especially from automation) you want to have custom options, or paths depending on the type of build that is being run, or if there are things you want to choose at build time rather than hard-coded into your build script.

The short answer is, you cannot.

The reason is that Unity will not let you inject data/information into the build process directly or has a parameter to your build method (e.g., ***BuildProject(string overridePath, bool buildAssets)***); however, where there is a will, there is a way.

While we cannot inject parameters in the build, we can customize our build script to **READ** the parameters that the Unity command was launched with, so instead of passing parameters, we can just append them to the Unity.EXE command and get them from there instead.

To accomplish this, we need to add a special function into our Unity Build script to be able to read these command-line parameters.

Listing 8-3. Utility to get command-line arguments

```
// Helper function for getting the command line arguments
private static string GetArg(string name)
{
    var args = System.Environment.GetCommandLineArgs();
    for (int i = 0; i < args.Length; i++)
    {
        if (args[i] == name && args.Length > i + 1)
        {
            return args[i + 1];
        }
    }
    return null;
}
```

With the helper in hand, now you can append your Unity build execution with additional options:

```
Unity.exe -projectPath <unityProjectPath> -logfile <logFilePath>
-batchmode -nographics -quit -executeMethod Builder.BuildProject
-outputPath <buildOutputPath> -buildTarget <yourBuildTarget>
-myCustomOption1 myValue1 -myCustomOption2 true
```

And then read the values back in the build script as follows:

```
string myCustomOption1 = GetArg("myCustomOption1");
bool myCustomOption2 = bool.Parse(GetArg("myCustomOption2"));
```

Now you have the additional options you wanted available in your build script to do with what you wish. It is a bit of a hack, because Unity, but it works.

P.S. You can also use this method for a Runtime Unity project, so if you wanted to add a "-noSteam" or other arguments and have your game initialize differently, you can ☺.

Addressables

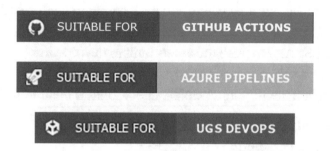

By default, Addressables are only built manually in your Unity project using the Addressables Editor windows, which can be a pain. However, we can also modify our build script to include a command to force build our addressables assets when we build the project.

We simply need to add the code in Listing 8-4 in the build script, likely after the **BuildPipeline.BuildPlayer** command, so we do not do the extra step until a full build has been completed (also worth checking that the BuildResult was also positive) but BEFORE "EditorApplication.Exit".

Listing 8-4. Addressables build script command

```
if(buildReport.summary.result == BuildResult.Succeeded)
{
    try
    {
        AddressableAssetSettings.BuildPlayerContent();
    }
    catch (Exception ex)
    {
        Debug.Log($"BuildPlayerContent Crashed - {ex.StackTrace}");
    }
}
```

It is that simple; just tell Unity to build it. Following this of course, you will have a whole set of compiled Asset data that needs to then be uploaded to your CDN (Content Delivery Network) or storage area where you have configured addressables to pull the asset from. For this, you should use the best path offered by the vendor, either an Azure Upload Task or a REST API, to push the assets built in the pipeline.

For more information about Addressables, check Unity's documentation:

```
https://docs.unity3d.com/Packages/com.unity.
addressables@1.21/manual/index.html
```

Building UPM Packages

UPM is an interesting beast for Unity; it affords the ability to produce immutable packages that you can include in your project without the pesky issue of it corrupting and polluting your main Assets folder; you will have used these from time to time, especially as it is now the primary shipping method Unity uses for all its features.

What most developers fail to recognize is that we can do the same thing with our projects, portioning off foundational or fixed elements to their own packages and having just the core elements within our main Unity project; I have used this process repeatedly with many projects from large to small, as well as having the ability to completely reuse packages across many solutions. Have a set of utilities, prefabs, and components you are constantly reusing, package them in a UPM package, and just keep adding them; there is a level of discipline you need to adhere to for any reusable feature, but Unity actually makes that fairly easy to manage (as a package is immutable and cannot change).

When creating UPM packages, you have several patterns in which to maintain them:

1. In a solitary repository, with nothing but the UPM package (my personal preference)

2. In a repository with a blank Unity project, with the package located in the "Packages" folder

3. Simply as a folder in your Unity solution within the Packages folder

Each has their own pros and cons, mainly around maintenance and reusability. With option 3, it becomes much harder to reuse the package as it is contained within your project and is not "by default" read-only. Options 1 and 2 require additional maintenance, and changes do require additional effort as they are separate.

Personally, I use a combination of 1 and 3, using the repository for the UPM package as designed, but then creating submodules (Git projects within Git projects) in my project's "Packages" folder when I need to make changes (although you can leave them there, but can then be prone to accidental modification). By default, however, I add my package repository using a Git URL package through the Unity Package Manager, mainly to protect it against change.

This is something I highly recommend experimenting with when building your project as it has huge advantages.

How this fits into an automation title is that if you use option 2 or 3, where the UPM package is still effectively part of the project, it is just in the Packages folder instead of the Asset folder, so there is nothing more to say about them.

With option 1, we hit a small "snag," as it does not have a Unity project to build with. To solve this, we simply need to script in a process to

- Package our package into its own folder

- Generate a new Unity project on the fly

- Put the package into the "Packages" folder of the temporary Unity project

- Build/test/etc.

The beauty of this is that it all happens during the build/test cycle, and the additions are not committed back to the repository, we are just checking everything is good and working, and if you are smart (and intend to possibly sell/publish the package later), validate it on all the versions of Unity and platforms you wish to support. For instance, the Unity UI Extensions project I maintain is built and tested against seven versions of Unity on four platforms; without automation, this would take the better part of a week every time I made a change.

You can see the automation build for the Unity UI Extensions project here:

`https://github.com/Unity-UI-Extensions/com.unity.uiextensions`

It should come as no surprise that UGS DevOps **does not support building UPM packages on their own**; they MUST be included either as a submodule or copied into the Packages folder of another Unity project.

What Are Unity UPM Packages

A brief note on what makes a Unity UPM package – they are (in short) NodeJS packaged projects (Unity used a standard for a change ☺) and have a fairly simple structure.

You can read about the structure in more detail here:

`https://docs.unity3d.com/Manual/CustomPackages.html`

All that is really needed from the preceding specification is the following:

- A "**Package.json**" (manifest) definition for the project

- A "**Runtime**" folder containing all the runtime scripts, components, prefabs, and anything else

- An "**Assembly Definition**" file in the Runtime folder to contain their scope

- *(Optional)* An "**Editor**" folder containing all the editor scripts, components, prefabs, and anything else

- *(Optional)* An "**Assembly Definition**" file in the Editor folder to contain their scope

Everything else is purely optional, like samples, documentation, tests, and so on. For personal projects, I do not usually bother (except for tests, one must always test 😂).

The manifest can also be very simple, only putting in what you need, for example, see Listing 8-5.

Listing 8-5. Package.json example

```
{
  "name": "com.[company-name].[package-name]",
  "version": "1.2.3",
  "displayName": "Package Example",
  "description": "This is an example package",
}
```

All the rest is "fluff" and descriptive which you only need if you intend to publish your package to a store, like OpenUPM (the home of MANY free Unity UPM packages).

Check out OpenUPM here:

`https://openupm.com/`

When creating packages just for myself, I like to keep the effort to a minimum; alternatively, I use a package generator which does most of the work for you (including adding sample tests); these can then be customized, which you can check out here:

- `https://github.com/SimonDarksideJ/Unity-Package-Sample`

Building and Testing UPM Packages

The first step in building the workflow (once you have the code from the repository cloned, you do need the code after all) is to build a custom script to simply do the tasks listed earlier, for example, see Listing 8-6.

Listing 8-6. Example UPM project creation – GitHub Actions

```
name: Build UPM PAckage

on:
  workflow_call:

jobs:
  run_build:
    name: Package UPM for test
    steps:
      - uses: actions/checkout@v3
        with:
          submodules: recursive
          clean: true

      - id: package
        name: 'Run Unity Builds'
        run: |
          $UPMFolderName = 'u'

          if ( -not (Test-Path '$UPMFolderName') )
          {
            New-Item $UPMFolderName -ItemType Directory
          }

          Move-Item -Path * -Destination $UPMFolderName -exclude $UPMFolderName

          $TempUnityProjectName = 'P'
```

```
Start-Process -Verbose -NoNewWindow -PassThru -Wait -FilePath
"C:/Program Files/Unity/Hub/Editor/2022.3.0f1/Editor/Unity.exe"
'-createProject' $TempUnityProjectName -quit

$destinationPath = Path.Combine($TempUnityProjectName, 'packages')

Move-Item -Path $UPMFolderName -Destination $destinationPath
shell: pwsh
```

The example is written for GitHub actions; however, the custom script will work for any platform, such as Azure Pipelines; being a custom script, it is fairly interoperable for any vendor. The script executes like this:

1. Define a folder for the UPM package.

2. Check if that folder already exists (rare but can happen) and create the folder if it is not found.

3. Move the contents of the cloned UPM package repository into the new temporary folder.

4. Run the Unity editor command passing the arguments "**createProject**" and "**-quit**" to create a temporary Unity project.

5. Create a path to the Packages folder inside the new temporary Unity solution.

6. Move the temporary UPM package folder to the Unity project's Packages folder.

The preceding script assumes you are using Unity 2022.3.0f1 and that it is installed in the default Unity install location, and you may need to change the path yourself. If you look at the build scripts in the Unity UI Extensions project mentioned earlier, there is a **LOT** of boilerplate added to work with the Unity Hub and Unity editor in order to work with any version and install location and on any platform (the above also only works on Windows).

The GitHub actions build script made for Chapter 11 also includes this if you want to reuse it.

Following the script in Listing 8-6, you can then run any normal Unity Build/Testing Extensions/Actions upon it to validate the package does what it is intending to do.

This is more advanced, and (as mentioned earlier) you can simply use Git submodules (or script cloning other repositories to your packages folder) to also achieve the same. However, my recommendation stands for almost any sized project:

- Put crucial/reusable elements of your project into a separate repository as a UPM package.

- Add that repository as an "Add Git URL" UPM package to your project.

- Only clone the UPM package to your project packages folder when you need to make changes (then remove and refresh the package).

- Build as normal, as Unity will import the Git URL packages the same as any other package.

This keeps your project safe, keeps reusable code safe and maintained properly (no unintended changes that could affect other projects using the same package), but still gives you the freedom and ease to update the project WHEN REQUIRED.

In some projects, I have maintained the UPM packages completely separately for safety, including Tests Scenes solely for those packages in a Development-only project that includes all UPM packages maintained by the project. You can see there here in the Reality Toolkit solution which is for building cross-platform XR solutions. Pay close attention to the "Packages" folder of the project and ALL the UPM packages that are maintained by it (we just use the packages themselves for creating/publishing solutions):

https://github.com/realitycollective/realitytoolkit.dev

Publishing UPM Packages

If you do decide to publish your UPM package, it is also very simple through automation; in fact, the only hard part is updating version numbers, which you can do manually or use NPM packaging tools to do it for you. Ultimately (for services like OpenUPM), you simply need a "tag" in your repository corresponding to the release or just use the raw branch itself (not advised for "published packages").

Listing 8-7. Tag and release custom script

```
- name: Publish package tag
  if: ${{inputs.createTag == true}}
  run: |
    $outputVersion = '${{steps.getpackageversion.outputs.
    packageversion }}'
    git tag -fa "v$outputVersion" "${GITHUB_SHA}" -m "v$outputVersion
    Release"
    git push origin "v$outputVersion" --force --tags
  shell: pwsh
```

Excerpt from the "upversionandtagrelease.yml" script from the Reality Collective:

```
https://github.com/realitycollective/reusableworkflows/blob/
main/.github/workflows/upversionandtagrelease.yml
```

The preceding script simply

- Takes an input version (in the preceding example, sourced from an earlier part of the workflow)

- Tags the current state of the Git repository with that version (prefixed with "v")

- Pushes the new tag up to your repository for use

The tag effectively creates a pointer to a specific state of your code; future changes will not affect it. Most solutions (like OpenUPM) will read this tag and create a published package from it for users to consume.

If you used option 2 in the list of patterns described earlier in this section and still wish to publish your package, you will need to do what is called a "Git subtree split" to separate out the folder in the Packages folder into its own branch or repository in order to consume it in Unity; thankfully, GitHub itself provided some easy steps for doing this, and you can implement them using a custom script in your automation if you wish:

```
https://docs.github.com/en/get-started/using-git/splitting-a-
subfolder-out-into-a-new-repository
```

UPM Summary

That was fun, was it not 😈? Something I highly recommend if you want to maintain good clean projects.

If you thought that was fun, we now head into darker waters to handle those platforms that just cannot help themselves, and Unity washes its hands of them as soon as it can (unless you are doing "build and run," which in some instances Unity just refuses to do, for no good reason).

Onward travelers.

Two-Pass Building for Strict Platforms

Some platforms need additional effort in order to actually get a buildable/deployable solution out of them, namely, Windows 10/11 and iOS (although it is becoming more critical with Android too these days); once you get the output from Unity, you then have to do a manual (and sometimes painful) task to actually run it. When it comes to automation, this is its bread and butter; doing the tasks you would prefer not to, however, using automation also adds a few little quirks (enforced by the platforms).

To make matters worse, information on how to do this effectively is scarce to find or out of date, communities are not always "helpful" (you should know this, else you cannot be "one of us"), and trial and error can be painful (some weeks of my life I will never get back), but thanks to this title, you will get the benefit of my many hours of research and testing for the quick and easy path. You are not alone, as I have often freely shared these insights on various automation channels, but you will be the first to get it in written form 🦴.

Secrets and Other Files

We covered secrets in Chapter 4 and everything needed to record them; I will also go over them again in Chapters 10 and 11, but we will include more here, mainly because in almost ALL cases, there is information you should **NEVER** make public or even publish in a private repository, else it could potentially lead to disaster; this can range from

- Certificates (both for encrypting and publishing)

- API keys and uber secret values

- Your mother's maiden name, the street you grew up on, etc.

When building for some platforms, these things are almost always needed and should not be written down or "kept safe somewhere" because they only have a single use, generally to be able to ship your project out the doors and into the consumer's hands safely.

I have lost count over the decades of instances where "secrets" have been added to public repositories, a "secure file share," or put on sticky notes in a safe; they are almost always found out and in the worst cases can have disastrous consequences for you and your business. Best to treat them like your most favorite possession and keep them close.

For Mac, this ranges from certificates from your build machine, API keys, usernames, and passwords; for Windows, usually it is just a certificate. If you are also using external systems like Networking (Photon?), API access, and so on, then you may need to keep those too, then through automation inject the "real" keys into the build. In development, you should ONLY test with development/test keys to keep things safe, and if possible, do not check those into source either (exclude them in your *.gitIgnore*).

I mention it here just to reiterate what has been said already and note that when the instructions call for one, know where you have stored it!

Certificate Storage

When it comes to storing certificates within the respective platforms, there are a few subtle differences, although the end result is the same; you need to store

- The certificate file (contents)

- The password for the certificate

- The SHA/thumbprint for the certificate (validation check to ensure the cert has not been tampered with)

These are stored as follows:

- Azure

  https://learn.microsoft.com/en-us/azure/devops/
  pipelines/library/secure-files?view=azure-devops

  Azure allows you to upload the certificate itself and "tag" additional variables against the file which are then bundled together with the "**DownloadSecureFile**" Pipeline task; this can then be read by any subsequent task that needs to access it.

- GitHub

  https://docs.github.com/en/actions/security-guides/
  encrypted-secrets

  Things are a little more complicated in GitHub as it does not yet have the same facility as Azure; instead, you must **Base64-encode** the contents of any certificate (to avoid symbol issues) and store it in a GitHub Actions Secret; to use it in subsequent actions, you must decode the string from Base64, alongside additional secret values in separate parameters.

Building for Windows

If you are just building for Windows Standalone, you can just move on, nothing to see here, mainly because the default Windows build that Unity does is sufficient and creates an executable that you can zip up or package in an installer to deploy. You might want to inject your secrets into the build, which we are not covering as there are too many variations.

But for Windows 10/11 native applications, or for deploying to Windows ARM/HoloLens devices, you need to do a separate build step using the MSBuild tooling.

You can read about the full scope of MSBuild tooling using the following link; we will only be covering what we need to know to build for Windows. P.S. Unity also uses MSBuild for most platforms, except iOS.

```
https://learn.microsoft.com/en-us/visualstudio/msbuild/
msbuild?view=vs-2022
```

When you build locally using Visual Studio or some other tool, most of the MSBuild execution is handled for you, including adding certificates, the build, and final compilation, but through automation, as it is command-line driven, we must do most of the heavy lifting ourselves. Where it gets tricky is that no one tells you what arguments to use when running the tooling for specific scenarios, and while Visual Studio does generate output when doing build, it is not always clear.

A certificate is required for a Windows build, which is generated within the Visual Studio project that was built by Unity, the instructions for which can be found here:

- ```
  https://learn.microsoft.com/en-us/windows/msix/package/
  create-certificate-package-signing
  ```

  With the certificate generated, you simply need to upload it to the secure file area for your automation using the details provided earlier; once complete, you will need to make it available within your workflow, either using the "DownloadSecureFile" task in Azure pipelines or decoded from the GitHub Actions Secrets where it is stored.
  ```

- Azure

  ```
  https://learn.microsoft.com/en-us/azure/devops/
  pipelines/tasks/reference/download-secure-file-
  v1?view=azure-pipelines
  ```

- GitHub

  echo "${{ secrets.CERTIFICATE }}" | base64 --decode > <certificate_file_name>

With the certificate available, you can then use an MSBuild task/action to take the built Unity project and turn it into an actual Windows build, using the certificate to bundle it, as shown in Table 8-2.

Table 8-2. *Using the MSBuild task/action to transform a Unity project into a Windows build*

Azure Pipelines	GitHub Actions

- task: DownloadSecureFile@1
    name: signingCert
    displayName: 'Download CA certificate'
    inputs:
    secureFile: '$
(certdetails.securefilepath)'
 	
- task: VSBuild@1
    name: BuildUWPPackages
    inputs:
    solution: '$
(Build.BinariesDirectory)/UWP/**/*.sln'
    platform: 'ARM64'
    configuration: 'MasterWithLTCG'
    createLogFile: true
    msbuildArgs: '/p:AppxBundle
    Platforms="ARM64"
 	
/p:AppxPackageDir="$(build.
BinariesDirectory)/UWP/AppxPackages/"
 	
/p:UapAppxPackageBuildMode=
SideloadOnly
 	
/p:AppxPackageSigningEnabled=true
 	
/p:AppxBundle=Never
 	
/p:PackageCertificateThumbprint=
"$(certdetails.thumbprint)"
 	
/p:PackageCertificateKeyFile=
"$(signingCert.secureFilePath)"
 	
/p:PackageCertificatePassword=
"$(certdetails.password)"'
	- name: Add msbuild to PATH
	uses: microsoft/setup-
	msbuild@v1.1
	
	- name: Build app for release
	run: |
	echo "${{ secrets.
	CERTIFICATE }}" | base64
	--decode > $(Build.Binaries
	Directory)/certificate.cert
	msbuild "$(Build.Binaries
	Directory)/UWP/**/*.sln" -t:
	rebuild -verbosity:diag
	-property:Configuration=Release
	-property:AppxBundle
	Platforms="ARM64" -property:
	AppxPackageDir="$(build.
	BinariesDirectory)/UWP/
	AppxPackages/" -property:
	UapAppxPackageBuildMode=
	SideloadOnly -property:
	AppxPackageSigningEnabled=true
	-property:AppxBundle=Never
	-property:PackageCertificate
	Thumbprint="$(secrets.
	thumbprint)" -property:
	PackageCertificateKeyFile=
	"$(Build.BinariesDirectory)/
	certificate.cert" -property:
	PackageCertificatePassword="$
	(secrets.password)"

Provided you have created all the secrets correctly, variables on a secure file in Azure, or three secrets in GitHub (cert, thumbprint, and password), should produce a build which you can then zip up and publish elsewhere.

If all else fails, try, try, try again.

Building for Mac/iOS/iPad

Things on the Apple side of the farm are a little trickier, mainly because of all the hoops that Apple makes developers jump through to get onto their most exalted platform.

I am not going to go into exhausted detail in this section, mainly because it would take an entire book to do so. I am however going to detail the critical parts, give you some workflow examples, and then point you to some of the best tutorials on the Web to get the specifics. I am however (for once) going to assume that you have at least some Mac knowledge and understand the terms; if not, then you are in for a rough ride, as Apple expects it.

If you are new to Apple development, create a free account and check through their getting started docs for app building/deployment, which will give you an understanding of the requirements. My recommendation is to only start on your Apple journey if it is your only platform, or get to it as your last, making sure everything else is working and building BEFORE attempting Apple, just saying.

The setup basically comes down to a few specific parts:

1. Access to a Mac, hosted or self-hosted (due to the complexity, I have always used self-hosted as it is cheaper and easier to manage).

2. Apple developer account (goes without saying, but it is the only platform that MANDATES it, even just to build).

3. A team registration on the Apple Developer Portal, either organizational or personal based.

4. App registration on the Apple Developer Portal.

5. Access to a Mac, either hosted or local. No getting away from it, you need access to a Mac somehow, if not for builds, then for generating the requirements to start building, namely, a certificate.

6. The rights/permissions on a Mac to generate certificates and access the keychain, mainly administrator access.

7. A mobile provisioning profile for the development environment, generated either from the self-hosted agent or generated from tools on a Mac.

8. An "**info.plist**" predefined with all the options for the application.

These requirements are the same whether you are building via Azure Pipelines or GitHub actions; they are simply the critical components to build on a Mac. You may find through testing that "automatic provisioning" works well if you try and build the app manually; however, for automation (in my experience) this either does not work or does not produce a workable build; a Mac is and continues to be a pain in my side whenever I have to resort to building for it.

I'm not anti-Apple, but it is the most troublesome platform to build for and, worse, get support for when things go wrong; I can only hope it improves in the future (it just never has for me in over a decade).

The process for building for Apple with everything in place is as follows:

1. Generate the Unity build, configured with as many of the settings as possible (I find it smooths things if Unity has all the same settings configured).

2. Create a build, which will output an Archive (xcarchive) that is ready for distribution. (This builds the Xcode project.)

3. Archive the build which generates the final application (.ipa) that can be distributed to either a device or to the Apple Store/ TestFlight.

Each step will test you as you build it, and then once it is working, try and never touch it again.

The hardest things I had to get right were the arguments to use for steps 2 and 3 earlier, which are as follows.

The Xcode Build Command

Listing 8-8. Xcode Build command (remember to swap out values)

```
xcodebuild -project '$(Build.BinariesDirectory)/<project folder>/
Unity-iPhone.xcodeproj' -scheme Unity-iPhone -configuration 'Release'
-destination 'generic/platform=iOS' -UseModernBuildSystem=YES clean archive
-archivePath './$(Build.SourceBranchName)_$(Build.BuildId).xcarchive'
DEPLOYMENT_POSTPROCESSING=YES DEVELOPMENT_TEAM='<Your Apple Dev Team ID>'
-allowProvisioningUpdates DEBUG_INFORMATION_FORMAT=dwarf-with-dsym GCC_
GENERATE_DEBUGGING_SYMBOLS=YES ENABLE_BITCODE=YES
```

The Xcode Archive Command

Listing 8-9. Xcode Archive command (remember to swap out values)

```
xcodebuild -exportArchive -archivePath './$(Build.
SourceBranchName)_$(Build.BuildId).xcarchive' -exportPath
'$(Build.ArtifactStagingDirectory)' -exportOptionsPlist
'$(Build.BinariesDirectory)/<project folder>/info.plist'
-IDEBuildOperationMaxNumberOfConcurrentCompileTasks=8 -jobs 16
-allowProvisioningUpdates -allowProvisioningDeviceRegistration
PROVISIONING_PROFILE='<project provisioning profile ID>' CODE_SIGN_
IDENTITY="iOS Distribution"
```

These commands were based on Azure Pipelines, but it is easy enough to swap out the environment variables for ones used by GitHub.

Additional Resources

While the above is not 100% enough to get you up and running, there are some resources I have relied upon and have kept up to date with when it comes to modernizing building with Apple; you always have to be on your toes as Apple (in all honesty) almost requires you to keep using the latest and greatest to stay ahead of the times, which would not be so bad if it didn't cost $0000000s to stay up to date.

These are (at the time of writing) the best articles for each of the respective platforms:

- Azure: `https://medium.com/objectsharp/building-ios-application-using-azure-pipelines-92918080af9`

- GitHub Actions: `www.andrewhoog.com/post/how-to-build-an-ios-app-with-github-actions-2023/`

Both assume you are using hosted agents, but it is very easy to switch to self-hosted as a Mac is always a Mac (until Apple says it is not).

I wish you well and hope the additional information will give you more help than I have ever had trying to get builds working on a Mac.

Two-Pass Building Summary

As you can see, some platforms add that little bit of flavor when it comes to getting a build out of the door, and the list appears to be growing, so you need to keep on top of things (recently, I had to apply the same strategy for Android, but it is not common, yet).

UGS DevOps do have some solutions for building for iOS (not for Windows 10/11 UWP), and the Android options are limited, but here is hoping they improve things moving forward. All their documentation on their site is current, so it is not worth repeating here as it would likely be out of date by the time the book is published.

Stay tuned for Chapter 9 (up next) for an in-depth tutorial on navigating through Unity Gaming Services – DevOps.

Distribution

Your project is built, the testers have gone through it, and you have fixed all the bugs (that you have found); now you are ready to unleash your project onto the world (even if it is only a preview). Again, this is where automation can be a big help, at least when you have done all the leg work to get registered, paid all the fees, and told the publisher you are going to actually send them a game.

Granted, most studios and developers I have talked to usually prefer to do their first release manually; it is a stressful enough time without the added complexity of putting automation in the mix; they get their builds that have been output and then take the final leap themselves. You do not have to, and possibly by your second project, you will be more comfortable with the machines taking over....

Unity Gaming Services does stand out in this regard, as their "Distribution" platform is well thought out and supports about ten platforms; however, this does not include Apple deployment, Google Store, the Windows Store, or Steam, which are some of the more popular app destinations. But it is worth investigating.

Thankfully, there are many options using Azure Pipelines (which ChatGPT recommended for Unity UGS builds 🐟) or GitHub actions for most of the popular destinations.

Azure Distribution

Of the many extensions for distribution using Azure pipelines, these are some of the most common extensions:

- Apple Distribution – Provided by Apple, these are pre-built extensions for working with Apple delivery; of note, the "AppCenterDistribute" is very robust (once you have all the API keys configured) for delivering to either TestFlight or the Store.

- Google Play – Like Apple, Google also publishes its own "Google Play Task" for uploading a build to the Google Play Store; it is quite efficient and, once set up, easy to maintain.

- Custom scripting – Most other providers usually provide an API for which to connect to in order to deploy a build, so it is worth checking their documentation for more details. For instance, Steam recommends using "SteamPipe" to upload your build automatically.

GitHub Actions Distribution

- Apple Distribution – Apple provides a service called "**FastLane**" (which is used by the Azure Pipelines Task), for which there are many extensions on the GitHub Marketplace that utilize it for Apple deployments to the Store or TestFlight; the dependencies are a little more severe, but all of the actions are well documented and supported. Just take care when choosing and work out if it is suitable for self-hosting if that is your path.

- Google Play – As with everything on GitHub actions, for almost anything you want to do there are a multitude of community actions to do the task, and Google Play is no different; all you do is run the action with your build "aab" (Google build) and your keys and off it goes, uploaded directly.

- Steam – GameCI (you will learn more about it in Chapter 11) has a pre-built task for Steam distribution; just give it the keys and off it goes. There are also a few other "Steam Deploy" tasks available on the GitHub Marketplace (if you recall, I stated that GitHub had more add-ons than Azure).

- Many, many more – If there is not an action available already, like with Azure, you can script it using the vendor's public API. But with GitHub actions, there are many more options available, and if there is not one and you build it, then there is an opportunity to get your name in lights and publish one!

Summary

And so, we come to the end of the theory and discussion, talking about all the high and low points of what it takes to be an automation superstar. I did prewarn you this was a heavy chapter, and you may want to refer to this on occasion to help you through a sleepless night.

As we lean toward the end of the title, let us now turn to action and have a go at utilizing the services we have been discussing. We are not going to cover EVERYTHING we've discussed in theory as I do need to leave you something to work out yourself (and also keep this title under the size of an encyclopedia), but you will have more than enough to ensure that with each of the platforms you have all the workings to take your Unity project and get it built and tested through automation. If you decide to go further using this chapter, I wish you well in your adventure.

CHAPTER 9

Setting Up Unity Gaming Services Automation

As stated previously, Unity Gaming Services (UGS) offers a quick and easy-to-use automated build system, and while it might not be as full featured or as powerful as some of the more dedicated solutions, for a lot of projects it provides a quick and robust solution for testing/building and delivering Unity projects, granted, at a cost (there is NO free tier, although some subscriptions do include Unity Build Server, allowing you to run automation on premise).

Prerequisites

To get started with Unity Cloud Build (much like all automation), you will need a couple of things first:

1. A source control repository

2. A Unity project in the repository

© Simon Jackson 2023
S. Jackson, *Accelerating Unity Through Automation*, https://doi.org/10.1007/978-1-4842-9508-3_9

1. Source Control

One thing that UGS requires, much like all other automation solutions, is a Unity project uploaded and maintained from a source control system that UGS supports, which includes the following fully integrated solutions, such as

- Plastic SCM (Unity's own source control system)

- GitHub

- Bitbucket

- GitLab

- Azure Repos

It also contains base integration with other source control solutions based on (which you have to set up manually)

- Git

- SVN

- Perforce

Effectively, UGS supports all of the most common offerings available. Granted, there is a lot of push and preference to use Plastic SCM, Unity's own offering, but so far, I have not seen anything that is superior to other integrations, other than having a single dashboard to manage everything.

Plastic SCM does include a free tier for (tiny) projects managed by three people or less, and beyond that, you are paying again.

Unity version control (Plastic SCM)

For those working on projects with multiple team members across various roles who need to collaborate on large filesets and binaries while minimizing lost work and overly technical tooling. Start free with a shared repository hosted in the cloud. If you need an on-prem solution, contact sales to get started.

	Free	Pay as you go	Enterprise
	For small teams	For growing teams and projects **Free usage included**	For large studios that need an on-premises server. Contact sales to get started
Active users	Up to 3	Up to 3 free then 4+ users, $7/user per month	$23/user per month (unlimited)
Cloud storage	Up to 5GB	Free usage and then 5-25GB, $5 per month 25+ GB, $5 per 25 GB	n/a
Self-hosted (On-prem)	No	No	Yes

Figure 9-1. Unity Plastic SCM pricing

Not much, but it still does not compare to the larger free options from other providers. It is completely up to you as to the path you choose for your studio.

2. You Need a Unity Project

Now while this might seem obvious, to build a project using automation requires the actual project that you want to build in source control. However, it is worth mentioning **how** you should make your project available; you can either

- Put your project in the root of your repository – which works fine with most source control "ignore files" to omit Unity's background folders like the Library, Temp, and Build folders.

- **(Recommended)** Put your project in a folder within the repository – Unity also supports building from a subfolder in your source control project, which is sometimes preferred by developers as it keeps the Unity parts of your project away from the source control files like ReadMes, git files, and such.

Just make sure the default Unity "*git ignore*" files are not targeting the *ROOT* of your source control folder, else you may end up with the extremely large and unneeded Library folder checked into source control, which makes downloading the project VERY long and will cost you pennies in your Unity Cloud Build; time is money!

Know the Costs

As the Unity build offering is not free and does not include any free time, it is important to understand the costs involved. These are quite minor and are offered on a "pay as you go" contract (only paying for what you use); however, you pay for EVERY build, regardless of whether it is successful or not.

COMPONENT

Unity Cloud Build

For Unity mobile and PC game developers, Cloud Build is a turnkey CI/CD solution that automatically creates performant and multiplatform builds in the cloud to deliver higher-quality games to market more quickly than ever. If you need an on-prem solution, learn more about Unity Build Server.

	Pay as you go For growing teams and projects
Target platforms	PC, WebGL, Android, Limited XR/VR, iOS/Mac
Automation minutes	Windows - $0.02/build min Mac - $0.07/build min
Automation OS	Windows & Mac

Figure 9-2. *Unity Cloud Build pricing*

As is quite common across all the automation providers, building on a Mac is more than three times that of building on Windows, so something to keep in mind as you develop, for example, get it running on all other platforms before you build for Mac 😊, unless iOS/Mac is your platform target of choice. As pricing goes, it is almost the same as other platforms, except for the lack of any free time.

Supported Platforms

At the time of writing, the Unity Cloud Build system only supports building for the following platforms:

- iOS

- Android

- Windows desktop

- Mac OS desktop

- Linux desktop

- WebGL

Building for Windows UWP or gaming consoles is not supported; for more details on these platforms, then get in touch with the Unity Expert Team:

`https://create.unity.com/contact-unity-expert`

Getting Started – Make a Project

As with all the offerings in the Unity Gaming Services bucket, such as Analytics/LiveOps (Live Operations)/Growth (marketing)/Monetization (advertising) and Multiplayer, the first thing you will need is a project, which you will create either when you first sign up or you can create an additional one from the Dashboard "Projects" view as shown in Figure 9-3.

Figure 9-3. *UGS Projects view*

You will also see any and all other projects you have created from this view, and thankfully there is no limit as to how many you can add, although you are billed "per project" for services that you consume, as well as getting paid "per project"; there is not a single portal (that I am aware of) covering all your projects and their performance (with the exception of ads).

By selecting to create a project, you get a very simple view which simply asks for the project name (Figure 9-4).

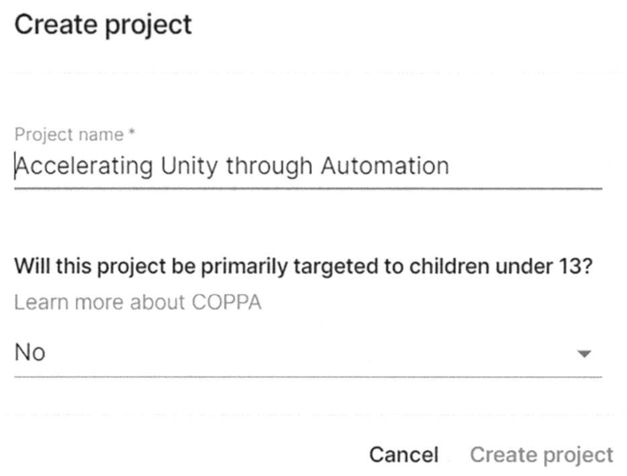

Create project

Project name *

Accelerating Unity through Automation

Will this project be primarily targeted to children under 13?
Learn more about COPPA

No ▼

Cancel   Create project

Figure 9-4. *New project view*

You are asked if the project is intended to target children, likely due to regulations regarding adverts, although I find it odd that Unity mandates this and does not just include it with their monetization setup; projects may choose to instead gain revenue through direct sales; this should not need to be mandated to record this with Unity, but I digress.

With the project created, you have a few more options you can fill in, again, mostly for Unity's benefit (unless there is a reason it helps Unity to know your Google License credentials?). But at least you can add a pretty icon to make the project more recognizable in the Unity dashboard (and no, it does not update any assets in your project), as shown in Figure 9-5.

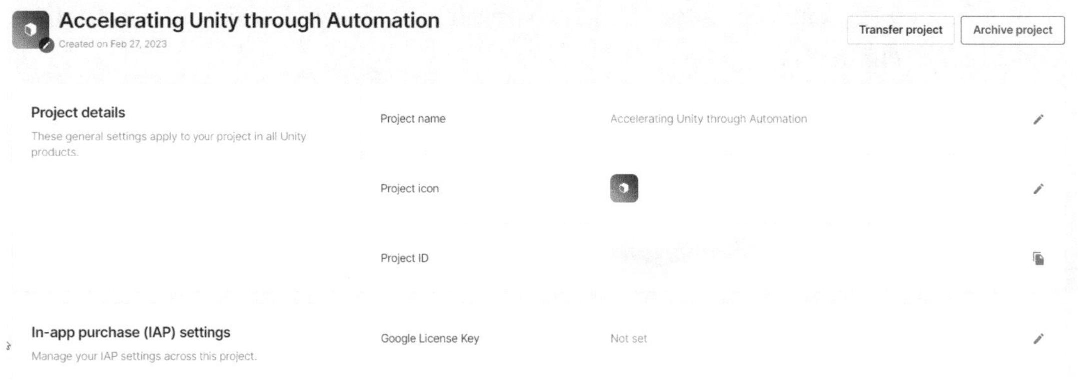

Accelerating Unity through Automation
Created on Feb 27, 2023

Transfer project   Archive project

Project details
These general settings apply to your project in all Unity products.

Project name   Accelerating Unity through Automation

Project icon

Project ID

In-app purchase (IAP) settings
Manage your IAP settings across this project.

Google License Key   Not set

Figure 9-5. *Project overview*

With your project created, we can get on to the actual task at hand, with building our project with Unity Gaming Services.

Registering for Unity Cloud Build

The first thing you will notice when entering the Unity DevOps area (unless you already have signed up) is the notice that you need to register to use Unity Cloud Build (Figure 9-6).

Figure 9-6. *Cloud Build registration prompt*

Fear not, registering does NOT cost you anything, you are only charged each month from when you start building.

By agreeing to "**sign up**," you are simply agreeing to a contract to pay for what you use in the future; Unity nicely reminds and prompts you what those costs will be before you agree (although it does lack the legal jargon regarding increases in prices during contract, but it is covered in the small print in Unity's general contract).

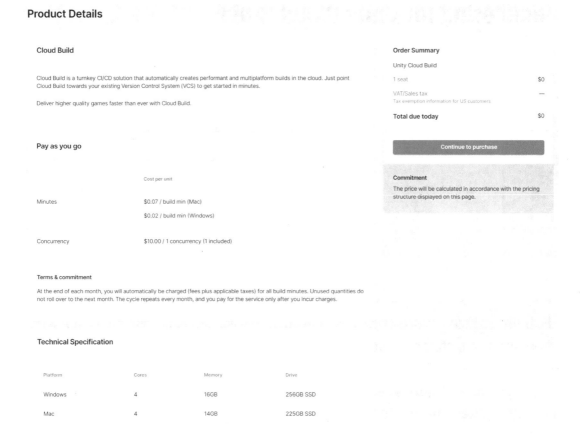

Product Details

Cloud Build

Cloud Build is a turnkey CI/CD solution that automatically creates performant and multiplatform builds in the cloud. Just point Cloud Build towards your existing Version Control System (VCS) to get started in minutes.

Deliver higher quality games faster than ever with Cloud Build.

Pay as you go

	Cost per unit
Minutes	$0.07 / build min (Mac)
	$0.02 / build min (Windows)
Concurrency	$10.00 / 1 concurrency (1 included)

Terms & commitment

At the end of each month, you will automatically be charged (fees plus applicable taxes) for all build minutes. Unused quantities do not roll over to the next month. The cycle repeats every month, and you pay for the service only after you incur charges.

Technical Specification

Platform	Cores	Memory	Drive
Windows	4	16GB	256GB SSD
Mac	4	14GB	225GB SSD

Order Summary

Unity Cloud Build

1 seat	$0
VAT/Sales tax Tax exemption information for US customers	—
Total due today	**$0**

Continue to purchase

Commitment

The price will be calculated in accordance with the pricing structure displayed on this page.

Figure 9-7. *Unity purchasing screen*

Once you pass through the gated checkpoints of Unity's standard purchases screen, your account will be ready to begin.

Thankfully, Unity does provide a handy guide for getting you started and a few documentation links to boot; as I have said before, it is a quick solution, and Unity has taken great strides to make it easy for you (Figure 9-8).

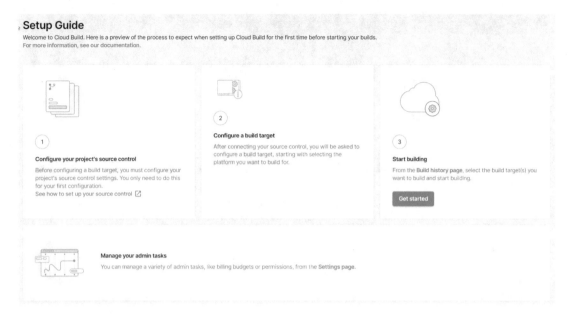

Figure 9-8. *Cloud Build setup guide*

From the Settings screen, Unity provides a handy link at the bottom of the page, from here you get an overview of where your project is, including the latest alerts and notifications (Figure 9-9) (although what purpose there is in telling you what browser you are using is beyond me).

Settings

General   Billing

Profile Info	Name	Simon Jackson
	Account	darkside@zenithmoon.com
	Billing Info	Please visit the Unity Online Store ⧉ to change your billing address and credit card details.
Additional Info	Server	dashboard.unity3d.com
	User Agent	Mozilla/5.0 (Windows NT 10.0; Win64; x64) AppleWebKit/537.36 (KHTML, like Gecko) Chrome/110.0.0.0 Safari/537.36 Edg/110.0.1587.56
API Settings API Documentation ⧉	API Key	
Automatic Build Sharing Enable or disable automatic build sharing. This will automatically create a share link when your build successfully completes. It will also populate notifications with the share link.	Generate Share Links	Disabled
Project Alerts When the "auto-build" feature is turned on in your project settings, Unity Cloud Build will build every time you commit to your repo. **This can result in high email frequency, especially for large teams.** This rule applies to **all members** in this project. If you only want to opt-out yourself, please change the **User Alerts** setting below	Project Email Notifications	Enabled
User Alerts If you don't want to receive the email notification for this project, you can disable this to opt-out.	User Email Notifications	Enabled

Figure 9-9. *Account settings*

The "Billing" tab, shown in Figure 9-10, is useful for letting you know what your bill will be at the end of the month, as well as setting spending caps or reminders to prevent your bills from getting too huge (although it does mean builds will stop).

Settings

General   Billing

Build minutes monthly cap ⓘ

To stay in control of your spending each month across Mac and Windows builders, you can set a dollar amount or choose to completely restrict your additional build usage with a $0 spend cap. This does not apply to storage or concurrency.

Mac: $0.07 / min
Windows: $0.02 / min

Status	Disabled
Dollar Amount	$0

Monthly cap reminder

Enable email notifications as you hit your build minutes monthly cap limit.

Status	Disabled
Dollar Amount	$0

Concurrency

All platforms: 1 concurrent build included, up to 7 additional for purchase at $10.00 each.

All **decrement** changes you make to your number of concurrent builds will be reflected in the following billing cycle.

Pricing information ⎘

Concurrency	1

Figure 9-10. *Account billing*

At this point, you have now passed the gatekeepers of Unity's services and may now proceed to make use of their offerings.

Connecting to Your Repository

With your Unity project in hand and your contract signed with a higher power, you are now ready to connect the dots and get your project ready to be built by Unity Cloud Build, which all in all is a quick and painless process. Unity does a good job of making the whole process quite seamless.

To begin, navigate to the "**Configurations**" tab in your DevOps dashboard (Figure 9-11), and you should see a welcoming screen just waiting for you to begin.

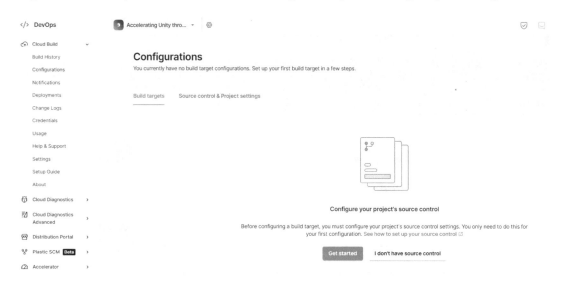

Figure 9-11. *Build targets configuration screen*

Clicking the "**Get started**" button will take you to the "**Source control & Project settings**" tab (Figure 9-12) and ask you to select a "**Source control provider**" (as listed previously in the "1. Source Control" section); if it is one of the integrated solutions, you will also need to "**Authorize**" your connection to your source control provider.

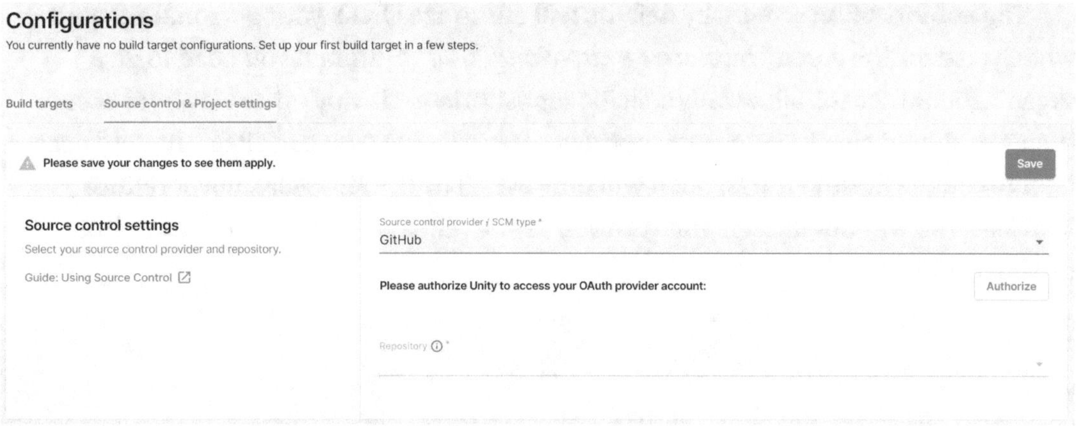

Configurations

You currently have no build target configurations. Set up your first build target in a few steps.

Build targets   Source control & Project settings

⚠ Please save your changes to see them apply.   Save

Source control settings

Select your source control provider and repository.

Guide: Using Source Control [↗]

Source control provider / SCM type *
GitHub   ▾

Please authorize Unity to access your OAuth provider account: Authorize

Repository ⓘ *   ▾

Figure 9-12. *Source control selection*

Note   This will likely use your currently logged-in account via a web browser, so check it is the right one before continuing.

For *GitHub*, the authorization screen will look as shown in Figure 9-13.

Figure 9-13. *GitHub account authorization*

The authorization screen, by default, will authorize ONLY your personal account when you click the green "*Authorize unity-cloudbuild*" button. If you need to give organizational access, allow only specific repositories or in any other way limit access, then you should check/change the options appropriately. You can "Reauthorize" access later to change these settings, but it will only ever INCREASE access, never reduce it, at least not without manual intervention in your GitHub or other source control provider setup.

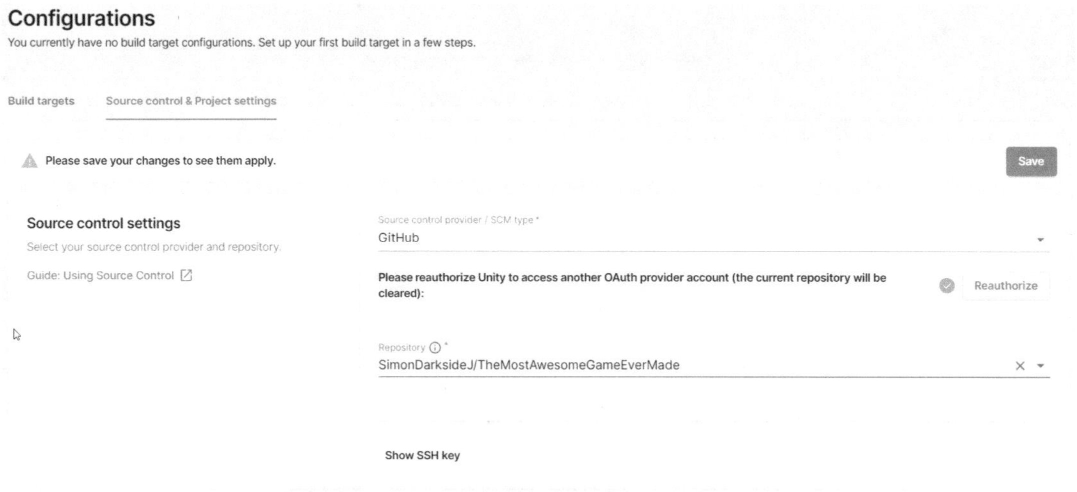

Figure 9-14. *Authorized GitHub account (with the "Reauthorize" button)*

A Note About Caching

By default, Unity will automatically cache the "*Library*" folder (Figure 9-15) for your Unity project, which is highly recommended, as this reduces repeated build times. Although, it also can cause issues if you are constantly swapping out dependencies and can create false connections in the "Library" folder. You can always **FORCE** Unity to do a clean build, but this is a manual operation, which will also clear out the cached Library folder; by default, however, the Library folder will remain.

Unity also gives you an option on the "**Source control & Project settings**" tab to change the caching default, should you require to cleanly build the cache every run.

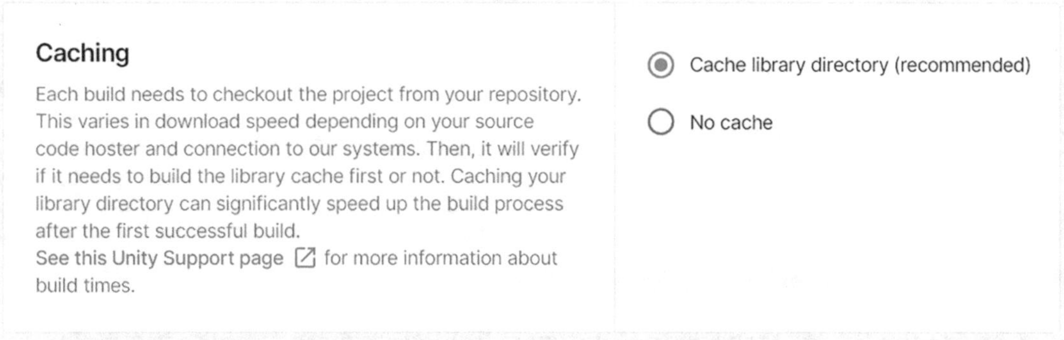

Caching

Each build needs to checkout the project from your repository. This varies in download speed depending on your source code hoster and connection to our systems. Then, it will verify if it needs to build the library cache first or not. Caching your library directory can significantly speed up the build process after the first successful build.
See this Unity Support page ☑ for more information about build times.

◉ Cache library directory (recommended)

○ No cache

Figure 9-15. *Library caching configuration*

Preparing for Builds

With your source control now set up and defined (assuming it is working), the "**Build targets**" tab (Figure 9-16) will now update to give you options to set up for which platforms you want Unity to build for (as listed in the "Supported Platforms" section).

Figure 9-16. *Build targets configuration*

Clicking the "**Quick target setup**" button will simply prompt you with the choice of platform to configure (Figure 9-17); this is just for a single platform, and you can add more later.

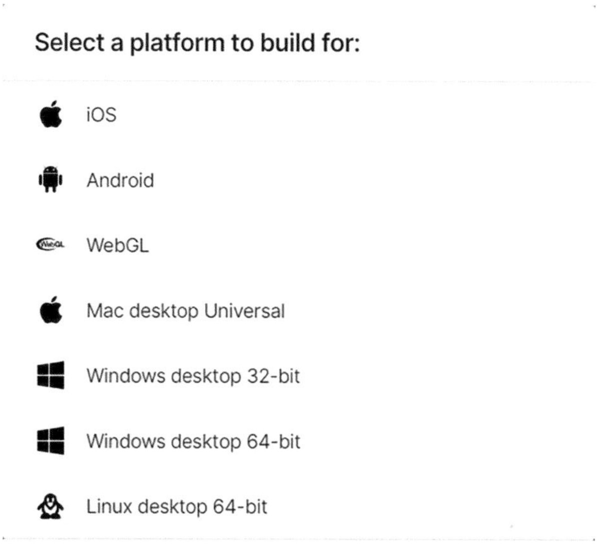

Select a platform to build for:

- iOS
- Android
- WebGL
- Mac desktop Universal
- Windows desktop 32-bit
- Windows desktop 64-bit
- Linux desktop 64-bit

Figure 9-17. *Platform build target selection*

With your platform selected, you then need to define from where your project is being built:

- Which branch to use

- The project folder, if your Unity project is NOT in the root of your repository

- The version of Unity to build for, either using the project's version or to automatically use the latest

- And which operating system to use to perform the build (see the "Know the Costs" section earlier)

Figure 9-18. *Build source configuration*

Note   WebGL and Linux builds are ONLY supported on a Mac currently, the most expensive platform to build on!

Android and iOS have special considerations for builds; make sure you check the *latest* documentation for details:

- iOS build options
  https://docs.unity3d.com/Manual/UnityCloudBuildAdvanced
  Options.html

- Android Build options – Docs do not exist, but the Android page does include links back to Google pages on what you need to configure for certificates.

Finally, you need to configure the scheduling options for the build, whether it is

- Manual – Simply do not configure any options.

- Automatic – Run when the source control is updated.

- (Optional) Auto-cancel – If your build is running, should the previous build be cancelled, or wait until it is finished before starting the next one. This will depend on your workflow and whether you need to test EVERY build or want to save time/resources/money and only have one build at a time (especially if one change was in error).

- Scheduled – Set an interval for which the build will run, either as a single (you can change it again later) or on a daily, weekly, monthly, or yearly schedule.

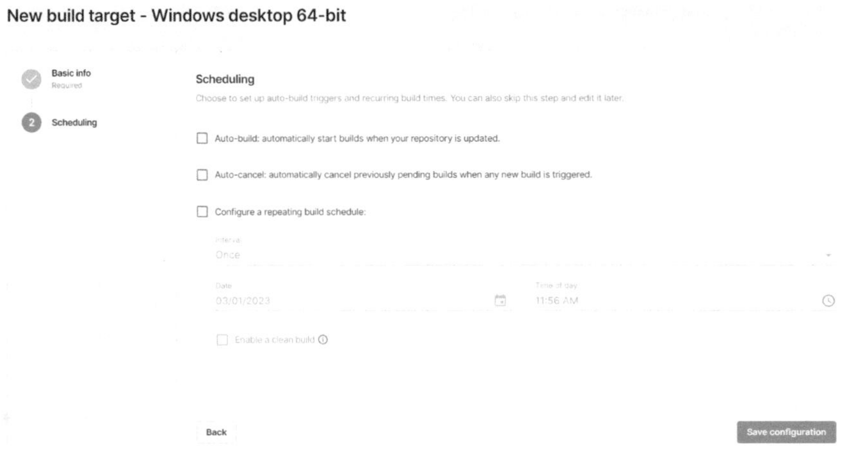

Figure 9-19. *Build scheduling*

Running Your Build

With a few extra build targets set up, your Configurations view will look something like what is shown in Figure 9-20.

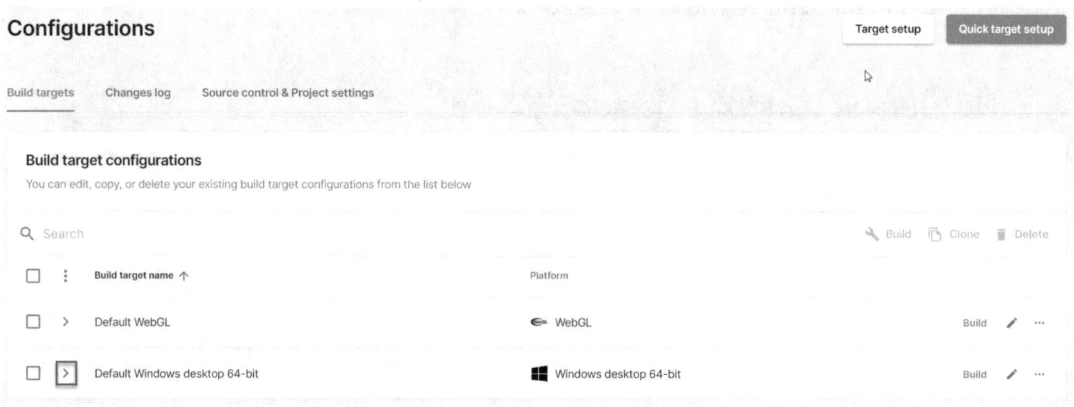

Configurations   Target setup   Quick target setup

Build targets   Changes log   Source control & Project settings

Build target configurations
You can edit, copy, or delete your existing build target configurations from the list below

Q Search   Build   Clone   Delete

☐ ⋮   Build target name ↑   Platform

☐ >   Default WebGL   WebGL   Build ✏ ⋯

☐ >   Default Windows desktop 64-bit   Windows desktop 64-bit   Build ✏ ⋯

Figure 9-20. *Build targets list view*

From here, you can edit your build target configuration; clicking the ">" symbol will also preview the basic configuration options listed earlier.

Clicking the "*...*" button will also give you a few additional quick options to clone (copy) a configuration, disable it from running, or simply delete it (does not delete any previous artifacts generated from the build, just permanently stops it running again). Figure 9-21 illustrates this.

Figure 9-21. *Build target quick options*

And for the astute among you, you will also see the "**Build**" option (which is not hard to miss as it is highlighted in blue, as you can see in Figure 9-22); clicking this will cause the Build to manually run and (hopefully) generate a Unity project. Optionally, you can also specify a specific commit message from which to pull the source, although it is not recommended to use unless you really need it.

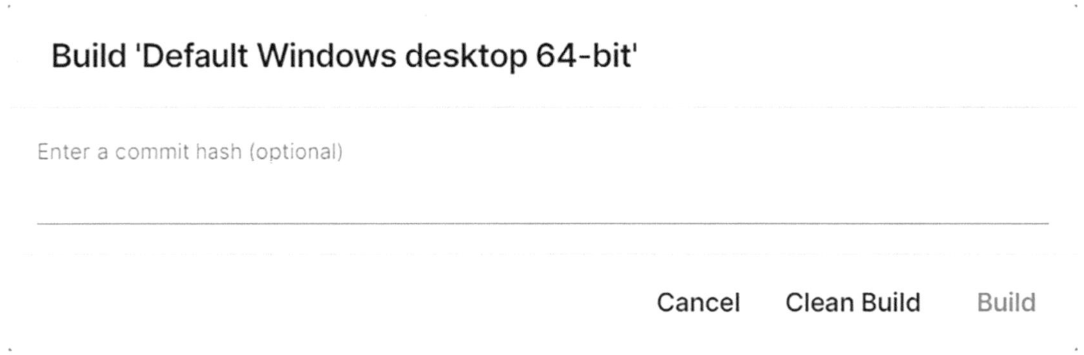

Build 'Default Windows desktop 64-bit'

Enter a commit hash (optional)

Cancel   Clean Build   Build

Figure 9-22. *Manual build message*

From here, you can " the build and even override the caching settings previously mentioned and force it to do a "Clean Build," wiping out any previous build's cache and building it fresh.

Once complete, you can view the results (Figure 9-23) of the build from the "**Build History**" tab and then download the build for testing on a device. You can also marvel at the full or compact logs to see how well your build is functioning (or know when it all goes wrong).

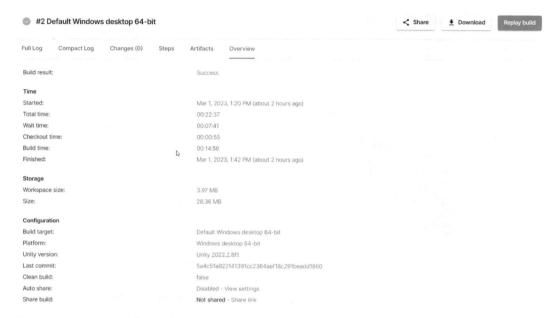

Figure 9-23. *Build results*

That is it for the basic operation of the Unity Cloud Build system:

- Create a project and upload it to source control.

- Create a build pipeline targeting the source.

- Make a build and download it when successful.

You also have a "Share" button to create a link to send to others so that they can also download the build securely.

If you want, you can try my build (Figure 9-24) on Windows:

`https://developer.cloud.unity3d.com/share/share.html?shareId=Z1tVFxeOfF`

You have until the year 2100 to try it, so best be quick!

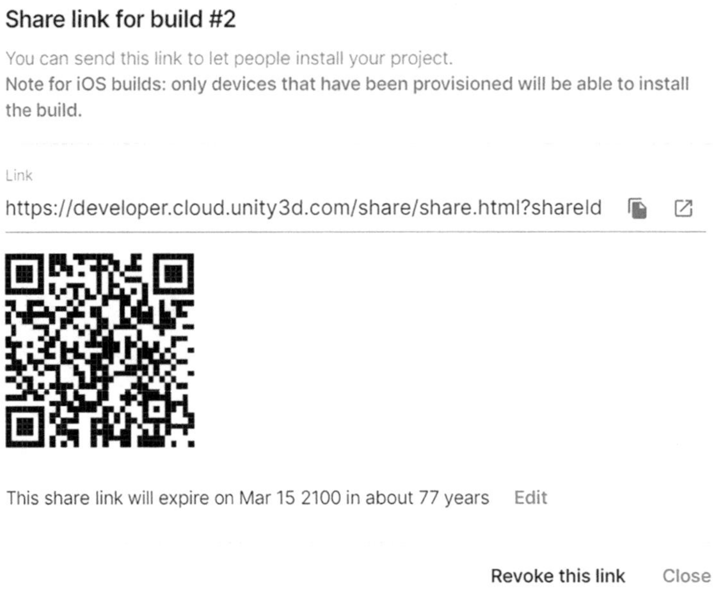

Share link for build #2

You can send this link to let people install your project.
Note for iOS builds: only devices that have been provisioned will be able to install
the build.

Link

https://developer.cloud.unity3d.com/share/share.html?shareId

This share link will expire on Mar 15 2100 in about 77 years   Edit

Revoke this link   Close

Figure 9-24. *The awesome game share link*

With the basics out of the way, what else can you do?

Advanced Build Options

Not to go into too much detail, but here are the "**advanced**" settings that Unity offers to
extend your Cloud Build solution; these can all be found in the "**Advanced**" tab when
viewing the configuration for a build, as shown in Figure 9-25).

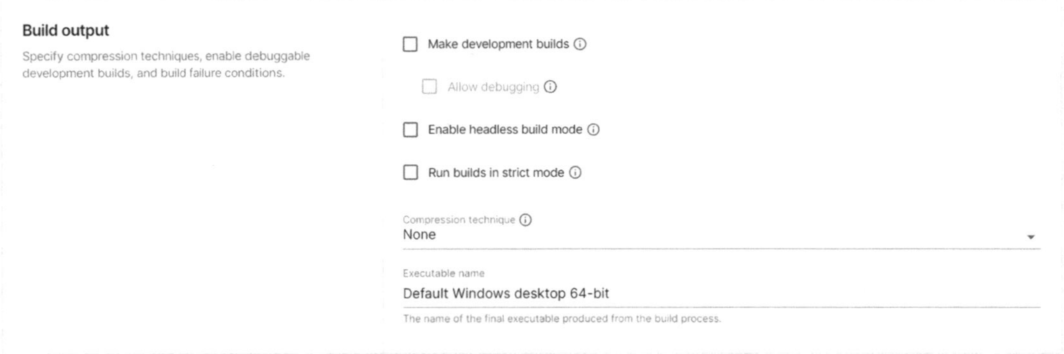

Build output

Specify compression techniques, enable debuggable
development builds, and build failure conditions.

☐ Make development builds ⓘ

☐ Allow debugging ⓘ

☐ Enable headless build mode ⓘ

☐ Run builds in strict mode ⓘ

Compression technique ⓘ
None

Executable name
Default Windows desktop 64-bit
The name of the final executable produced from the build process.

Figure 9-25. *Unity Cloud Build – Build output options*

Build Output

The first advanced option that Unity Cloud Build provides is probably settings that really should be part of the standard build options to be honest; they control things like

- A setting for enabling development builds, so debug versions of the project can be produced for additional testing, although, to be honest, this is far easier using a local copy of Unity; however, it is useful for issues that cannot be reproduced in a local build and only created with automated builds (even though it sounds the same, automated builds are different to local builds). Additionally, you can enable the "Allow Debugging" mode which allows developers to hook Visual Studio into the build.

- Even though this option has since been made obsolete, it is still available in Unity Cloud Build. Originally, it was for building console/server applications; however, with the enhancement of other Unity Cloud offerings, this is less useful these days.

- A useful option if nonfatal issues (such as shader compilation issues or missing reference errors) occur; by enabling the "Strict" option, this will cause the build to fail if ANY concerns are raised in the build. Ideally though, such issues should be ironed out in regular development, and I have not seen this option used in the wild, since it ends up costing more with builds that would likely be OK or fail due to known issues in third-party components.

- Builds, assets, and other components get compressed when you make a build; the "Compression" option lets you choose from a couple of options and, more importantly, allows you to disable compression if it is causing issues in your final build (but obviously increases the overall build size).

- The final option is fairly self-explanatory; it allows you to set the name for the final executable or program; by default, it uses the name of the Build action.

Note   Some options will change depending on the build target you choose; the preceding options are the full list of what is available.

OS Dependency

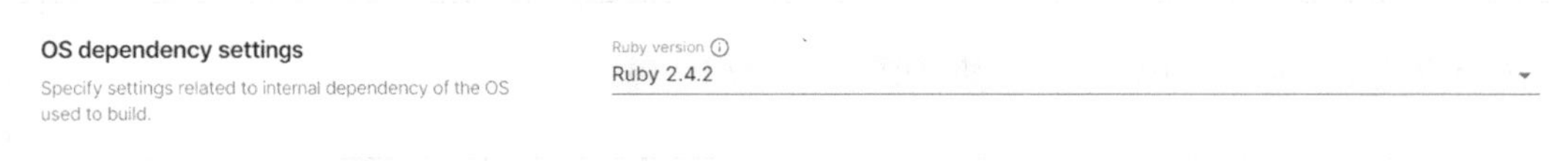

OS dependency settings

Specify settings related to internal dependency of the OS
used to build.

Ruby version ⓘ
Ruby 2.4.2

Figure 9-26. *Unity Cloud Build – OS dependency options*

The OS dependency options are more for iOS/Mac builds, allowing you to choose which version of Ruby (a web application framework) to use while producing the build. It does not have any effect on any other platforms (that I am aware of).

Script Hooks

Script hooks are Unity's way of enabling the extension of the build pipeline automatically (although it is also available in local builds); essentially, you can script additional things to happen **Before** and **After** a build takes place; what you can do with these scripts is up to you (Figure 9-27).

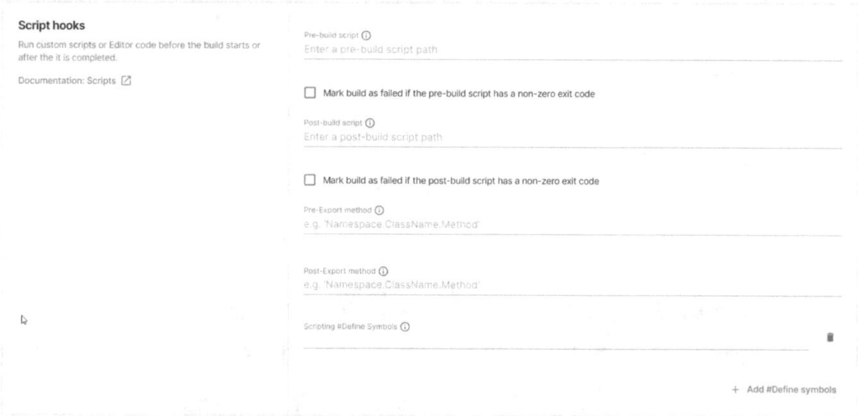

Figure 9-27. *Unity Cloud Build – Script hooks options*

Be aware When you use a pre- or post-build script, it will override any other options you or Unity provides to the build, meaning it will be only your scripts that run the build and not the normal Unity build process. This can be useful where you strictly need to control how a project is built based on code (rather than letting Unity do it), as well as the post-build tasks to upload built content (like addressables) to another host or upload the build logs to a secure site.

There is far too much to go into for this book, but something worth investigating if the default Unity Cloud Build options are not giving you enough flexibility.

There are several advanced options below that "can" be overridden using pre-/post-build scripts, just to make you aware in case you wonder why some options no longer work. The "rule of thumb" is to use **EITHER** the build script or the other options, but not both, in my personal view.

Environment Variables

The Environment Variables options (Figure 9-28) are the super advanced way to "tweak" how the Unity Cloud Build system handles your build; as you are effectively overriding the build behavior for the environment that Unity has provided, they should be used with **EXTREME** care.

Environment variables

Use environment variables if you want to dynamically give different configurations to your code for different builds.

Variable key ⓘ

Variable value

+ Add variables

Apply

Figure 9-28. *Unity Cloud Build – Environment variables options*

Personally, I believe these options are only available for Unity Build Server customers who may tailor their own internal build server differently to the Unity default, and I would NOT recommend touching these for using Unity's hosted servers!

These are for changing things like

- The install location for Android SDK/NDK
- The Home/Build directory that Unity will use
- Setting override build options like Verbose Logging, Unity Organization IDs, etc.
- Cloud Content Delivery (CCD) paths for publishing distributed content using Unity's cloud content system
- Fastlane options for Apple server publication

And a host of other options, you can read/see them all listed here:

```
https://unity-technologies.github.io/cloud-build-docs-public/
environment-variables
```

Tests

The "Test" options (Figure 9-29) are self-explanatory; if you have created unit tests (code written to test other code) in your project, then the Unity Cloud Build system will run these tests "prior" to running an actual build.

Tests
Determine conditions to run tests and take action on failures.

☐ Run my project's unit tests when building ⓘ

☐ Run EditMode tests ⓘ

☐ Run PlayMode tests ⓘ

☐ Mark build as failed if any test fails ⓘ

Figure 9-29. *Unity Cloud Build – Tests options*

Unit tests are extremely useful in situations where certain code MUST run in a certain way, else things will likely break, such as functions that should return true in a certain set of conditions, functions that return a value within a set range, etc.

Tests come in two forms:

- Editor tests (EditMode) – Code that is only run in the editor or effectively when the project is not running

- Run mode tests (RunMode) – Code that is expected to behave a certain way while Unity is running

Importantly, you have the option to pass or fail the build depending on the results of the tests. If the tests are more informative, just report on the state of the build, then you can still produce a running application. If, however, your tests are critical and the system will break if they fail, then the build should fail to prevent a more costly build process from eating cycles and costing you money for something you know will not work.

To learn more about unit testing in Unity, check out the Unity Test Framework here:

```
https://docs.unity3d.com/Packages/com.unity.test-framework@1.3/manual/
index.html
```

Scenes

Another self-explanatory option, which allows you to **OVERRIDE** the default scenes that will be included with your build, other than the build scripts, this is the only other dynamic way to alter what scenes are used when building your project (Figure 9-30).

Scenes

By default, Cloud Build builds the scenes you've added in the Build Settings menu of your Unity project. If you'd like to build a different list of scenes than what's in your project, add them here (as a relative path from the Assets directory).

Documentation: Scenes in Build

+ Add Scene(s) path

Scene(s) path

e.g. 'Assets/Scenes/Example'

Figure 9-30. *Unity Cloud Build – Scenes options*

This is extremely useful when you are targeting multiple platforms and you have specific scenes that are used for certain target devices, for example, a scene using low-poly art for mobile and a scene using high-quality art for console (although addressables are a better pattern for that); another option is if you have AR scenes for a mobile client and non-AR scenes for desktop. Ultimately, it all depends on your project and how it is built.

Setting the scene options here will **ONLY** affect the current platform being built for and no others; if left empty, whatever the default is set in your project is used.

Addressables

Addressables (Figure 9-31) are the modern way to handle distributed content for your Unity project; it provides many ways of handling the requirement for different assets for different platforms (such as low poly/high quality) or even using different assets/languages/content depending on how you implement it.

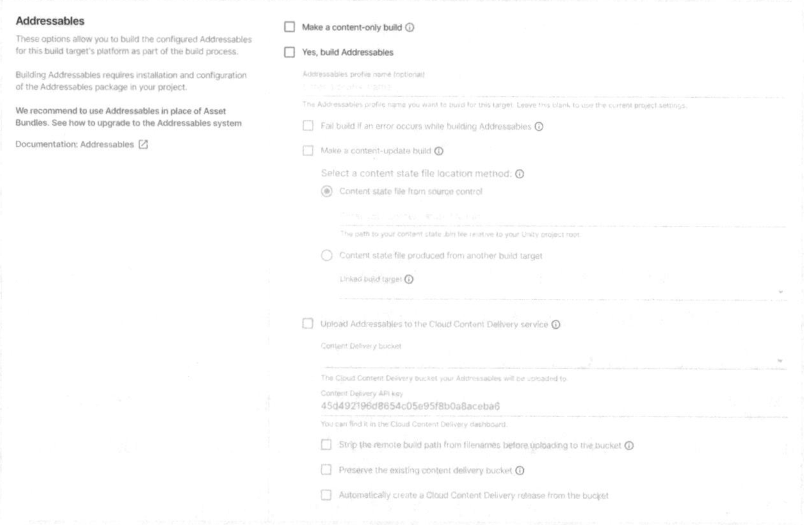

Figure 9-31. *Unity Cloud Build – Addressables options*

One small fact about Addressables is that they also INCREASE the management of the project, and if the same assets are used for multiple platforms, you will need to duplicate that content; it will not by default allow you to reuse content.

The options here allow you to customize where to publish the build content from the solution or even to make a "Content only" build if no code has changed (why build code if it has not changed). However, the options here are only supported if you are using Unity's Cloud Content system; it does not support publishing content to other hosts/platforms; for that, you will need a post-build script.

For more information on Addressables and their use, check out the documentation here:

https://docs.unity3d.com/Packages/com.unity.addressables@1.21/manual/index.html

Asset Bundles

Like Addressables are the new modern way to build content separate from your Unity project, Asset Bundles (Figure 9-32) are the legacy way. Unity is still trying to phase these out (although Asset Bundles are what are used behind the Addressables system anyway).

Asset bundles

These options allow you to build all configured Asset Bundles for this build target's platform as part of the build process.

If you choose to build Asset Bundles, an option to download built Asset Bundles will appear in the dropdown menu on a successful build.

Documentation: Asset Bundles ☑

ⓘ   We recommend to use **Addressables** in place of Asset Bundles to build assets. See how to upgrade to the Addressables system

☐ Make a content-only build ⓘ

☐ Yes, build Asset Bundles

Figure 9-32. *Unity Cloud Build – Asset Bundles options*

Asset Bundles are effectively packages of content that can be accessed at runtime and swapped out depending on the platform requirements (again, like the high-quality/low-poly switch). Within the Cloud Build system, Unity enables you to build your Asset Bundles within your project and, again, do a content-only build to reduce what is built.

To read more about Asset Bundles, check out the documentation here:

```
https://docs.unity3d.com/Manual/AssetBundlesIntro.html
```

Summary

That is the Unity Cloud Build system in a nutshell; it is quick and easy to use, has sufficient options to handle multiple platforms and multiple paths for building (making product builds or just content builds), and works best when integrated with other Unity-owned solutions (like Unity Cloud Content Delivery).

If you need more flexibility, then your only other option is to use build scripts, which means you are writing the build system (and mostly fighting with it) yourself.

But if all you need is quick and easy, Unity Cloud Build does a decent job, but every build will cost you.

Now that we are done with Unity, let us investigate some more flexible options. They may take a few extra heartbeats to learn but can offer a much more expansive option with more integrations that you can shake many sticks at.

CHAPTER 10

Setting Up Azure DevOps

Azure Pipelines is one of the original DevOps systems out there, beginning with automation built on top of Microsoft Team Foundation Server (Microsoft's original source control system); however, it was only after the introduction of GIT support that Azure Pipelines started to take off beyond its original enterprise beginnings. Today, it is a highly evolved ecosystem used by Microsoft itself to build the majority of its software today, all hosted on Azure, ensuring it is robust and has lots of resilience and support.

Let us dig in.

Prerequisites

To get started with Azure pipelines, you do not need much:

1. A Microsoft account (I would also recommend setting up an additional separate account to run the automation as well)

2. Your choice of source control repository, which can also be on Azure if you wish

3. A Unity project in the repository

© Simon Jackson 2023
S. Jackson, *Accelerating Unity Through Automation*, https://doi.org/10.1007/978-1-4842-9508-3_10

1. Microsoft Account

A primary Microsoft account is needed within the region you are registering for; this is used for billing, identification, and management of all Microsoft resources the account is responsible for. It does not have to be your personal account, it can be a separate account just for your organization. Later, you can add your personal account to the resources managed by the organization, so it does not interfere with anything else you have set up.

I also highly recommend setting up an additional account which will be used by the automation; this ensures it is secure, and any private keys required for the automation are owned and managed by this account (Personal Access Tokens often get invalidated with personal accounts and can wreak havoc with automation). It keeps things separate; it is cleaner and avoids additional risk and confusion. The automation account should also have its own access to the source control for the project (e.g., a GitHub account) to maintain the separation. Keep the account secure; enable 2FA (which you should have on everything anyway) and a random secure password (locked away for safekeeping).

This account is effectively going to be running your automation business for you, so keep it safe!

2. Source Control

There are many options for where you need to host your code (cloud automation does require your code to be cloud-hosted, somewhere), from Microsoft's own internal offering to GitHub and beyond, although Azure does support more types of source control options, such as

- Azure Repos Git

- Bitbucket

- GitHub

- GitHub Enterprise Server

- Other Git (any other provider based on Git source control)

- Subversion (the SVN method of source control)

Effectively, Azure supports all of the most common offerings available. Which you choose will ultimately be up to the organization or personal preference.

3. You Need a Unity Project

Like UGS, building a project using automation requires the actual project that you want to build is in a cloud-hosted source control system. However, it is worth mentioning **how** you should make your project available; you can either

- Put your project in the root of your repository – which works fine with most source control "ignore files" to omit Unity's background folders like the Library, Temp, and Build folders.

- **(Recommended)** Put your project in a **folder** within the repository – Unity also supports building from a subfolder in your source control project, which is sometimes preferred by developers as it keeps the Unity parts of your project away from the source control files like ReadMes, git files, and such.

Just make sure the default Unity git ignore files are not targeting the **ROOT** of your source control folder, else you may end up with the extremely large and unneeded Library folder checked into source control, which makes downloading the project VERY long and will cost you pennies in your Unity Cloud Build; time is money!

Know the Costs

Each Azure DevOps organization gets one parallel job with 1800 minutes (30 hours) of build time every month using Microsoft-hosted agents, which is A LOT; however, this cost is ONLY for when you are using Microsoft-hosted servers/agents; if you are using your own hardware, these costs do not apply.

There is no cost for using Azure Pipelines or the management system, only the resources you consume. See Figure 10-1 for details.

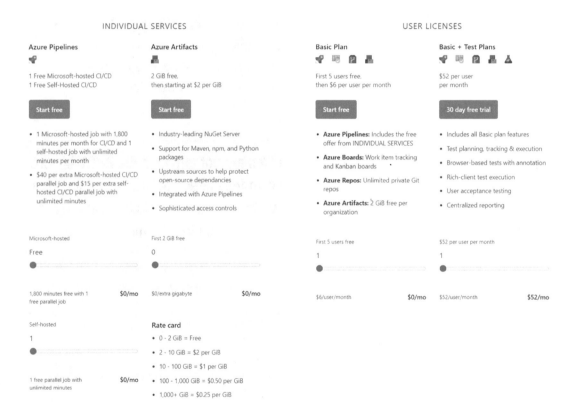

Figure 10-1. *Azure DevOps pricing*

As is quite common across all the automation providers, building using cloud-hosted Mac servers is higher than that of building on Windows, so something to keep in mind as you develop, for example, get it running on all other platforms before you build for Mac ☺, unless iOS/Mac is your platform target of choice.

However, if you have a spare Mac, you can install the Azure agent on it, and it just costs you the power to run it.

Supported Platforms

Azure itself does not limit building for any Unity platform; all you need is the server requirements to build it (whatever Unity supports through its editor) and the pipeline configuration to run it:

- iOS

- Android

- Windows desktop

- Windows UWP

- Mac OS desktop

- Linux desktop

- WebGL

- Xbox

- PlayStation

- Nintendo Switch (although there are several caveats)

- The new platform just released that Unity suddenly supports months later

Ultimately, there are no limitations; if you can build it on your Windows/Mac/Linux desktop, then you can build it in the cloud or on your desktop as a self-hosted agent.

Getting Started – Make a Project

Projects in Azure DevOps are simply containers for everything to do with a single managed project, be that an application, game, or even just a project plan for building something, it does not just have to be about code. Effectively, Microsoft is giving you the tools needed to scope out work to be done and facilities to manage the independent tasks required as well as mechanisms to follow those tasks through to completion (I have even used it to track class projects for students). But for the purposes of this title, we will be focusing on the automation parts.

If you want to learn more about the rest of the Azure DevOps features and capabilities, I recommend visiting the Azure DevOps learn pages here:

`https://learn.microsoft.com/en-us/azure/devops/pipelines/?view=azure-devops`

Once you have signed up to Azure DevOps using either a Microsoft or GitHub account from the main portal address here:

`https://dev.azure.com/`

you will have full free access to all the resources provided by Microsoft for Azure DevOps, including Azure Pipelines. If it is your first time accessing Azure Pipelines, you will be prompted to create your first project, which is the hub for all configuration, history, and facilities available for Azure automation, as you see in Figure 10-2.

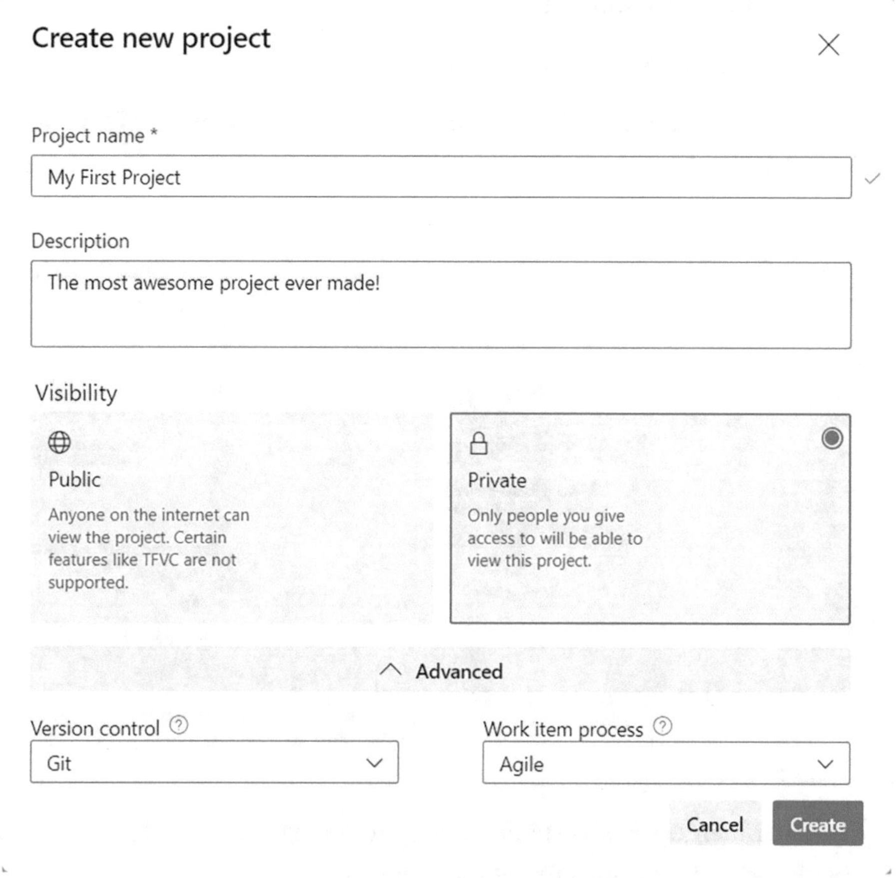

Figure 10-2. *Azure Pipelines new project creation*

If you already have an account/project, you can simply create a new one using the **"New Project"** button in the top right-hand corner of the Azure DevOps portal for your organization.

Once created, you will see the new home for your project that you have defined giving links for

- Managing members and giving access to others to your project

- Project management through Azure boards

- Linking repositories for source control

- Viewing test plans and test results

- Managing artifacts and resources for the project

But we will skip all that for now as we turn to focus on the subject of this title, Azure Pipelines (Figure 10-3).

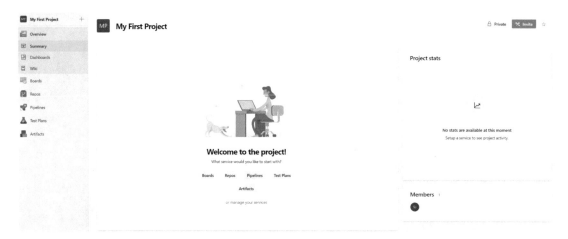

Figure 10-3. *Azure DevOps project dashboard*

Projects can either be

- Public – Meaning anyone with the URL to the project can access and view it (edit still requires further access)

- Private – Meaning only users with an account that has been granted access to this specific project can view it

Creating a Pipeline

Azure Pipelines (Figure 10-4) is the collection of tools to enable automation on the Microsoft Azure platform, integrating your code (wherever it is hosted), providing tools and capabilities to define an automation configuration and mechanisms to run those automations either on a scheduled or prompted activation. What sets Azure pipelines apart is that it has a focus on security and workflows designed around an enterprise's requirements, giving checkpoints and procedures to ensure that any costs that will be enacted using automation (if going beyond the free limits) are approved and checked. Not all these options have to be used, but they can be vital when mission-critical services are being made through automation.

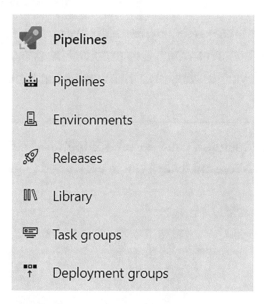

Figure 10-4. Azure Pipelines options

There are many facilities provided for the pipelines for a project (you can have as many as you need) including

- Pipelines – The automation workflows

- Library – The store for all pipeline-based configuration and storage for any/all secrets that are needed by the pipelines

There are also several capabilities aimed at web style deployment which are not in scope for this title:

- Environments – Environments are a collection of resources such as virtual machines or Kubernetes containers that pipelines can deploy to.

- Releases – A release is a dedicated pipeline holding all artifacts for a "release" before submitting it for deployment.

- Task groups – Task groups are an encapsulated set of tasks that can be executed in a deployment via a release pipeline.

- Deployment groups – A deployment group is a logical set of environments/hosts for which a release will be deployed to, for example, deploying a website to all machines in a cluster that host the website.

With your new project setup, if you select the "**Pipelines**" tab on the left it feels a little lonely in there, and Microsoft invites you to get started (Figure 10-5).

Create your first Pipeline

Automate your build and release processes using our wizard, and go from code to cloud-hosted within minutes.

Create Pipeline

Figure 10-5. New Pipeline prompt

There are several stages for creating a pipeline:

- Connection

- Selection

- Configuring

- Review

Connection

In the connection phase, you will specify the integrated source control system where your code is held. If you are not already authenticated with the provider, you will be asked to authorize your connection via the OAuth screen for that provider or create a new connection with the service as shown in Figure 10-6.

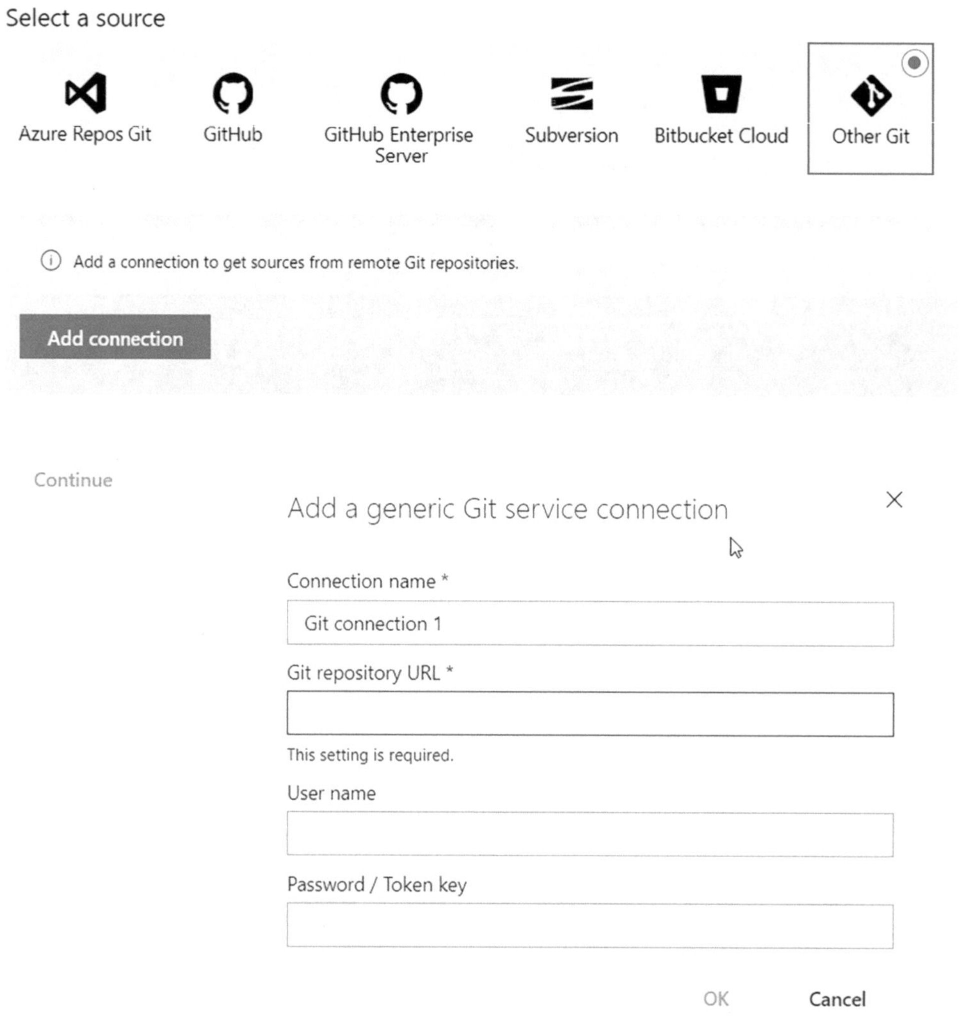

Figure 10-6. *Custom source control connection*

The options will change based on the requirements of each provider.

Selection

Once you are authenticated/connected, you will need to choose the repository you want to connect the pipeline to; be aware it will list **ALL** of the repositories the logged-on account has access to (Figure 10-7), so you may also need to use the filter options to narrow down the specific project, as well as switching to "All repositories" if the specific repository is not immediately visible.

This is why it is also beneficial to use a separate account for the source control access to limit the list of accounts/repositories the **Build Server** account has access to. If, like me, you have used MANY projects over your Git life, it becomes a very long list. 🧘

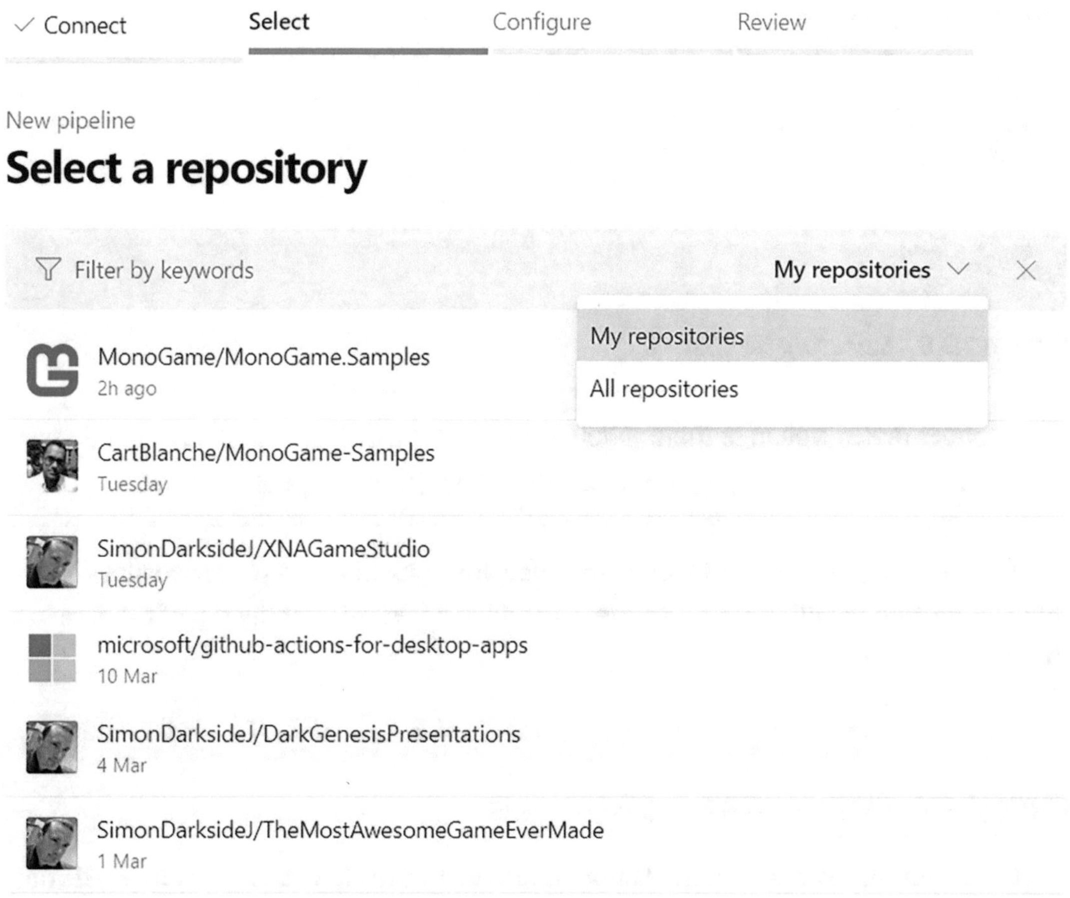

Figure 10-7. Repository list for the selected provider

Configure

With the repository selected, you now need to choose how to start your automation life, either making a new Azure Pipelines configuration or using an existing pipeline that is **already in the repository** (if you have made a pipeline outside of Azure or are reusing one from another project).

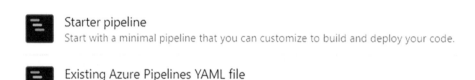

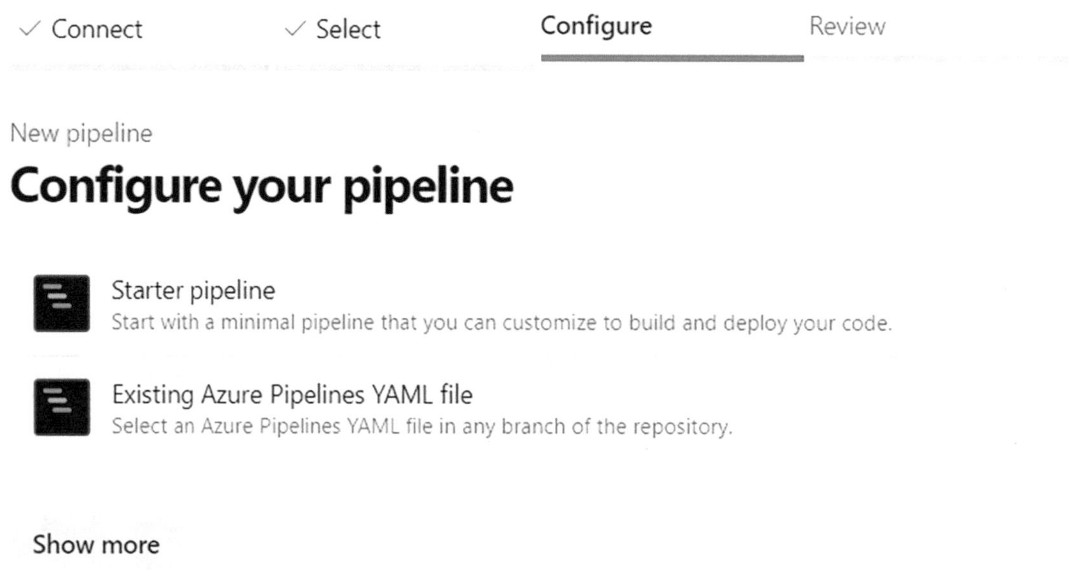

✓ Connect   ✓ Select   Configure   Review

New pipeline

Configure your pipeline

Starter pipeline
Start with a minimal pipeline that you can customize to build and deploy your code.

Existing Azure Pipelines YAML file
Select an Azure Pipelines YAML file in any branch of the repository.

Show more

Figure 10-8. *Selecting a pipeline*

The "Show more" option is there if you are creating a custom pipeline, such as a .NET build task or web deployment, so we can ignore that option for now.

If there is a conflict in the visibility between your pipeline and your repository, one set to public and the other set to private, you will see a warning at the top of the screen as shown in Figure 10-9.

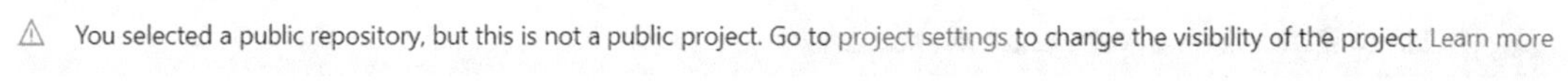

⚠ You selected a public repository, but this is not a public project. Go to project settings to change the visibility of the project. Learn more

Figure 10-9. *Pipeline access conflict warning*

This is nothing to be concerned about and is just warning you of the conflict; if you expect users of the repository to be able to see and access the pipeline, you will need to grant them specific access if it is set to private.

Review

On selecting the "**Starter Pipeline**," you will be taken to the Pipeline YAML editor (which we will cover more later) with a blank pipeline configuration, containing just enough to do "something" when run (Figure 10-10). By default, it will run a simple "hello world" script that will be executed on the "main" branch using a Microsoft-hosted Ubuntu agent.

Choosing "**Existing…**" will prompt you to select the specific YAML file from the repository and which branch it is located on.

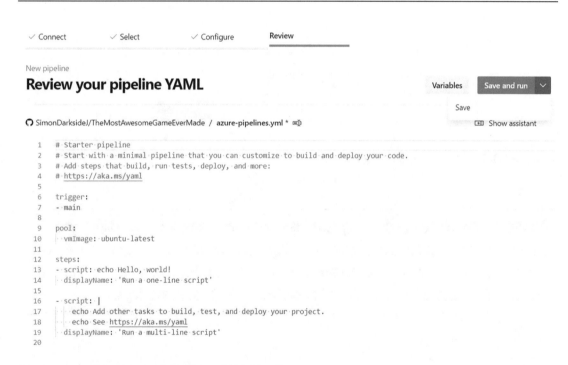

Figure 10-10. *Azure Pipelines YAML editor*

Finishing this step will "check in" a copy of the default YAML to a file called "**azure-pipelines-hosted.yml**" into the default branch of your repository (you can rename the file if you wish by clicking the icon next to the filename).

Clicking "**Save and run**" (Figure 10-11) will produce a prompt to let you control the check-in, with additional options to override the default branch and push the changes to a new branch if you wish, along with setting a message and description for the check-in.

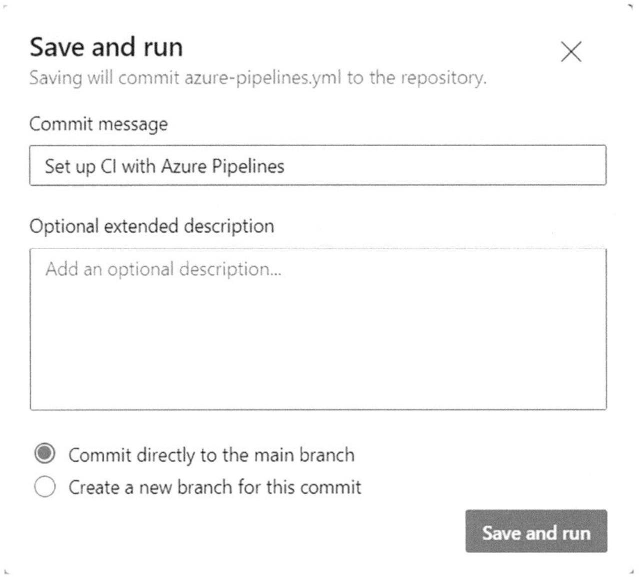

Figure 10-11. *Save and run prompt*

As you get more used to creating pipelines and operations, it is more likely you will use the alternate option of simply saving the pipeline and not executing it right away; to do this, click the downward arrow next to the "Save and run" button and select "Save" instead, which is what I do 99% of the time these days.

Executing a Pipeline

On every execution of a pipeline, it creates a "**Run**," which is a specific instance of the execution of the pipeline; every time a pipeline is run, either manually or automatically, it will create a new Run. The results and status of that run can then be viewed at any time.

If you selected "Save and run" in the previous step, Azure will automatically move to the Pipeline Execution details window, as shown in Figure 10-12.

Figure 10-12. *Pipeline execution result window*

If you do not see the window, simply click the "**Pipelines**" tab on the left, click your new pipeline, and then click the latest run to view it. But more on this later.

From this view, you can see the recent results of the pipeline execution including such details as

- Who ran it.

- Which repository it was run against, the branch, and even the specific commit details.

- The time and date it started, along with how long it took to execute.

- Any related work items if you are using Azure boards to track work; this will include any items that were covered or completed. You will also be provided with a link to any artifacts that were created and published for the workflow run.

- Any test results for the run, although this is not supported for Unity projects at this time, so we will ignore that for now.

- The results from any Jobs defined in the Azure Pipelines YAML for the run execution.

Clicking any Job result will then open a new window with the detailed results of the workflow execution, listing everything that was run for the job and the output that was generated. Figure 10-13 illustrates this.

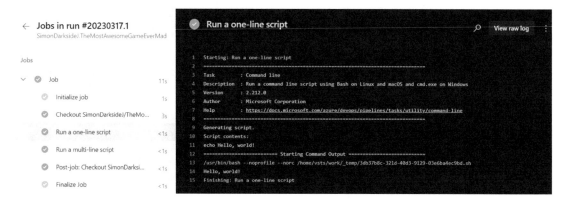

Figure 10-13. *Pipeline execution job run result window*

Clicking each line on the left will show you the output for each step along the way, from initializing the job, checking out the code, running tasks, and then finalizing and cleaning up.

You will know instantly if something did not work as there will be **RED** everywhere 👻, although figuring out what went wrong can take a little time!

Feel free to browse around and see what is what.

Automating Building Unity Projects

Now you have a basic understanding, let us now move on to the subject of building Unity projects using Microsoft's Azure Pipelines, for which we'll need a few extra things to help us along.

Ultimately, it comes down to two options:

1. Build it all manually yourself using scripting, endless nights of torture, far too much coffee (or other suitable hot beverages), and a far deeper understanding of just how much Unity helps you to build things (hint: it **DOES NOT**).

2. Stand on the shoulders of giants and use what has already been built. (This is my favorite option.)

For the sake of argument and not putting you asleep while reading this title, we will go with option 2 and install some Azure Pipelines extensions from the Azure Marketplace to make our lives a little bit easier.

Azure Marketplace

Being one of the oldest automation platforms, Microsoft Azure has an extensive collection of both Microsoft-built and community-driven projects available to address almost any task you could wish to undertake through your Azure automation; as an added bonus, the Azure Marketplace is carefully managed and maintained by Microsoft, so any extensions you find have been carefully vetted to ensure they do what they say they do.

When building Unity projects, the one extension that really stands out is the "**Unity Tools for Azure DevOps**" extension, written and maintained by Dino Fejzagić; it is one of the best available resources out there to get your Unity project built and tested.

Check *www.unitydevops.com/* for more details.

Installing extensions for your pipelines can only be done at the organization level, making the extension available for any project within your organization; to do this, click the "**Azure DevOps**" logo at the top left-hand side of the screen and then click/select the "**Organization settings**" option in the bottom left (Figure 10-14).

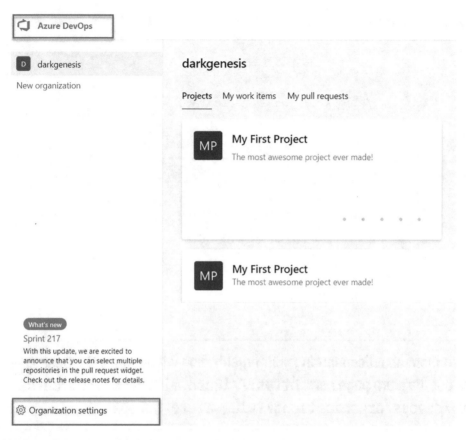

Figure 10-14. *Organization settings button*

Going into the Organization settings will fill your screen with a plethora of options, settings, and configurations for your entire organization; however, the only option we want right now is the "**EXTENSIONS**" tab (Figure 10-15) to see what we have installed and what we can install.

Figure 10-15. *Extensions settings*

To learn more about configuring your organization within Azure DevOps, please check out the learn page here: `https://learn.microsoft.com/en-us/azure/devops/organizations/?view=azure-devops`

Unless you have been playing with Azure pipelines previously, then the view should be as before, "blank and empty," so let us change that and install Dino's amazing tools to get the party started.

Click the "**BROWSE MARKETPLACE**" button in the top right-hand corner of the screen to get started.

A new window should open focused on all the marketplace extensions for Azure DevOps (you will also see filters for other products like Visual Studio, VSCode, and more). Figure 10-16 shows this.

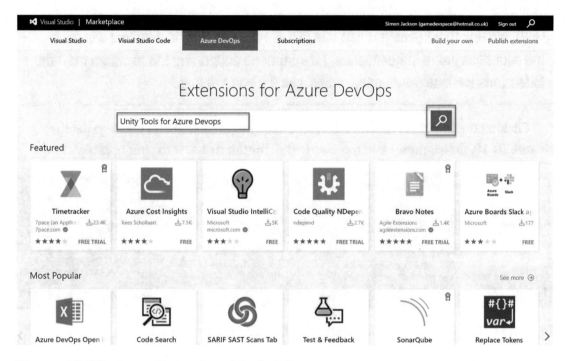

Figure 10-16. *Azure Extensions Marketplace*

By searching for "**Unity Tools for Azure DevOps**" and clicking the search button (or hitting enter), we should find the extension we are looking for, as shown in Figure 10-17.

Figure 10-17. *Unity Tools for Azure DevOps extension*

WAIT, what is that I hear you say, it is **FREE**. How can this be, this tool will save me countless hours of headaches! I recommend supporting the package from the Extensions website (www.unitydevops.com/) if you are able.

Clicking the search result will take you directly to the Extension package details (Figure 10-18, for example) and the Get/Install button to add it to your organization.

Figure 10-18. *Unity Tools for Azure DevOps extension details*

Now just click the "**GET IT** FREE" big green button and select your organization as shown in Figure 10-19, and you are all set.

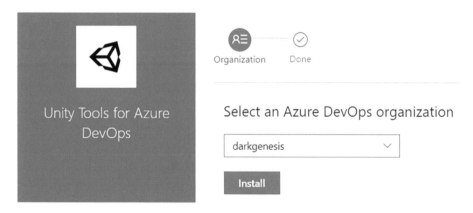

Figure 10-19. *Unity Tools for Azure DevOps extension install*

If you return to the "***Organization settings ➤ Extensions tab***," you will see the "**DevTools**" listed there now; there is nothing to configure, except to uninstall it (if you dare!).

Unity Tools for DevOps Extension

What does this extension give us? Here is a rundown before we start building a workflow to consume it:

- Get Project Version – This queries the Unity "**projectversion.txt**" file for the project and returns the version of Unity the project was last opened with. (This is needed in case you need to install a specific version.)

- Unity Setup – This will install a specific version of Unity onto the Build host for the automation, whether it is a Microsoft or self-hosted agent. If already installed, this will be skipped.

- Activate License – Mainly for when you need to activate a Unity Pro license on the host; this will register the installed version of Unity with a specific Unity ID user account and update the license. Not needed for Unity Personal unless you need access to specific Unity organizations for the build, for example, Unity Services.

- Unity Test – Runs Unity in "test mode" to run all the registered Unity Tests in the project. Any tests registered under the "***Window ➤ General ➤ Test Runner***" window will be executed. Results will be shown in the Run window for the pipeline.

- Unity Build – As the name suggests, this will run a Unity Build action for the selected project for a specific platform. Note, this is ONLY the Unity build and will generate Unity output; for platforms like Android and Windows, this will generate an executable project; for iOS/UWP, it will generate a project that will also need to be built separately to be run on a platform.

- Unity CMD – A custom action task to change Unity default options or run custom Unity scripts; for more details, check the documentation page for this feature (`www.unitydevops.com/docs/unity-cmd-task`)

As we update our starter workflow, we will tailor the preceding features to customize our pipeline to test and generate a Windows project; for others, you might want to join the **Unity DevOps** discord service to get further advice (`https://discord.com/invite/ RpHSpxkEP6`) or visit the documentation page for more details (`www.unitydevops. com/docs/`).

Putting It Together – Building a Unity Pipeline

As we reach the end of this chapter, we simply need to orchestrate the workflow to perform the tasks we need to build and publish our project; the flow looks something like this:

1. Get Unity Version – Get the version of Unity the pipeline is going to run for from the intended project.

2. Unity Setup – Check that the version of Unity required is installed.

3. (Optional) Unity Activation – If your project requires Unity Pro, then you will need to activate a Pro license in the automation. (Each Pro user comes with two activations.)

4. Unity Build – Create a build of the Unity project for the target platform, in this case, Windows Standalone.

5. Copy Task – Take the build created and move the built files to a staging area ready for packaging.

6. Publish – Create a published package for the staged items.

Note   Currently, Unity Personal licenses are only supported on self-hosted agents; Microsoft-hosted agents require Unity Pro at a minimum due to activation.

See the "Self-Hosting" section for getting the pipeline running on your own hardware under a personal license.

The YAML workflow looks like this:

```
trigger:
- main

pool:
  vmImage: windows-latest

steps:

- task: UnityGetProjectVersionTask@1
  name: unitygetprojectversion
  inputs:
```

```
    unityProjectPath: 'TheMostAwesomeGameEverMade/'

- task: UnitySetupTask@1
  inputs:
    versionSelectionMode: 'specify'
    version: '$(unitygetprojectversion.projectVersion)'
    revision: '$(unitygetprojectversion.projectVersionRevision)'
    installWindowsIL2CPPModule: true

- task: UnityBuildTask@3
  inputs:
    buildTarget: 'standalone'
    unityProjectPath: 'TheMostAwesomeGameEverMade/'
    versionSelectionMode: 'project'
    outputPath: '$(Build.BinariesDirectory)'
    outputFileName: 'TheMostAwesomeGameEverMade'

# Copy build output files to artifact staging directory.
- task: CopyFiles@2
  inputs:
    SourceFolder: $(Build.BinariesDirectory)
    Contents: '**'
    TargetFolder: $(Build.ArtifactStagingDirectory)
    CleanTargetFolder: true
    OverWrite: true

# Finally publish all items in artifact staging to the Azure Pipelines
# artifact storage. They will be available for sharing and/or further
# processing there.
- task: PublishBuildArtifacts@1
  inputs:
    PathtoPublish: $(Build.ArtifactStagingDirectory)
    ArtifactName: drop
    publishLocation: Container
```

We can inspect this using the Azure Pipelines YAML editor by returning to the
"**Pipelines**" view as before and clicking the "**…**" icon to the right of our pipeline and
selecting "Edit" as shown in Figure 10-20.

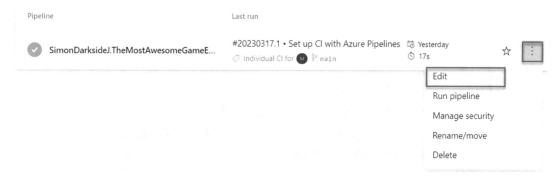

Figure 10-20. *Edit pipeline*

If you copy the preceding YAML into the editor, overwriting the previous starter template, we can walk through each of these options by clicking the "**SETTINGS**" option above each task, as shown in Figure 10-21.

Figure 10-21. *Pipeline "task" settings*

This will show up the friendlier GUI configuration for each task, highlighting additional, optional, and advanced options for each task (Figure 10-22).

Note   Not all tasks have a GUI configuration window; those that do not are usually script tasks. Refer to the documentation for each task for more details.

Figure 10-22. *Get Project Version Task*

Get Project Version Task

Only one option for the Get Project Version Task to set a child path for a Unity project. The sample project for this title has the Unity project in a subfolder called "TheMostAwesomeGameEverMade." *If your Unity project is in the root of your repository, this additional setting is not needed.*

Unity Setup Task

The setup task has the kind of options you would expect for installing Unity, ranging from which platforms to install as well as whether to install child modules (Android needs the Android SDK/NDK installing); see Figure 10-23.

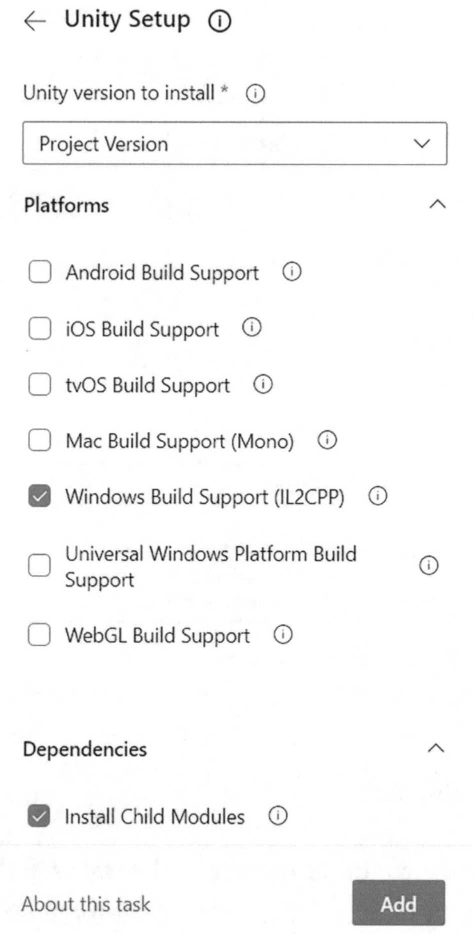

Figure 10-23. Unity Setup Task

Unity Build Task

For each platform you want to build for, you will need a Unity Build task (Figure 10-24). For example, if you want to build for Android, Windows, and iOS, you will need three separate Build Task entries which will be executed in parallel.

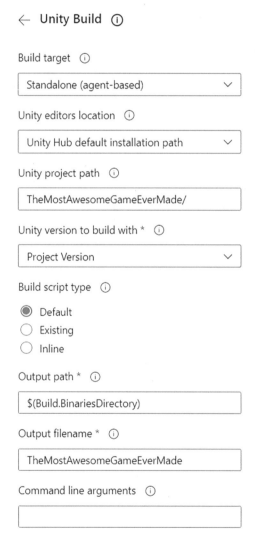

Figure 10-24. *Unity Build Task*

The options are pretty much the same as the other tasks in the Unity Build Tools. For details on the advanced options, check the online documentation or help provided with each argument/option.

Additional Tasks

The copy and publish tasks, while not necessary if you are just testing, are essential if you want the results of the build to be available elsewhere. Other publishing tasks may include

- Downloading certificates to sign your application/build

- Publishing to the Google Play Store

- Building the iOS/UWP project independently

- Publishing to the Apple Store/TestFlight

- Publishing to Microsoft AppCenter for Android/Windows delivery

And so on, extending and expanding your pipeline is fairly easy, although some (like Apple tasks) may take a little more trial and error to carve out parameters that meet the requirements for building/publishing. (Oh, the long-lost nights of tweaking Apple builds to make it compile and then publish.)

Self-Hosting

While building your actual automation is straightforward, tweaking it to meet your needs, while tedious, usually bears fruit to save you LOTS of time making and testing your builds, but the fact remains that if you are using hosted environments provided by third-party vendors, you will be eventually paying a premium to do so (like Unity Cloud Build). There is another option however; with Azure Pipelines, it is completely free to host your own agents on your own hardware, provided you have hardware/cycles to spare.

This can range from

- Using developer machines while they are not in use (overnight builds)

- Using hardware not currently in use, say if someone is on holiday or away

- Finding a spare piece of kit left over from an upgrade or simply collecting dust

The only requirement is to have hardware that is capable of the same tasks you would normally do for builds; it does not have to be quick or even have a lot of resources because at the end of the day, it is just running the builds in the background. It can even be your regular PCs as the operations are run in the background; all that happens is the machine will slow down a bit (or a lot depending on a build) while it is running (except for Mac builds; these have their own requirements).

Also, bear in mind that you are not limited to just using self-hosted or Microsoft-hosted agents, you can mix and match the automation to serve your needs.

Some workflows can be simple using minimal resources on hosted agents with ease, while more dedicated and resource-intensive tasks should use your self-hosted resources to keep costs down.

Self-Hosting Requirements with Azure Pipelines

Simply put, for a host to support self-hosted builds, it must have

- A dedicated user account that can access BOTH the PC in question and the Azure automation.

- The operating system to support a specific build operation, Windows for Windows/Android/Web builds, Mac for iOS/Android/Web builds, etc.

- The required software to run the build, for example, Unity, required SDKs, etc.

- Permanent access to the Internet; it is a cloud operation at the end of the day, and Azure needs to send builds to the machine.

- The required scripting support and libraries for automation, usually GIT, NodeJS, PowerShell, Bash, or a combination of each (which will depend on your workflow).

- POWER - The machine will need to be on for the times when automation is required.

The environment should be the same as any other development machine, and there is no limit to how many you can have; in fact, if the machine is powerful enough, you can install MANY agents on the same host to improve concurrency. The choice is up to you – several machines, each with the ability to execute a single build, or a bigger machine to run many.

Configuring an Azure Pipelines Agent

Once you have the machine setup for executing your builds normally, usually by cloning the project to the machine and running a build manually, just to grease the wheels, you can begin; any additional software requirements will make themselves known as you start running your automation by logging failures in your Pipeline log.

With your machine ready, you first need to decide whether the agents you set up will be solely for a single project or for any pipeline in any project across the organization; with that in mind, either navigate to

- *Project Settings ➤ Agent Pools*

- *Organization Settings ➤ Agent Pools*

The view is the same for both; all that is different is the scope and which pipelines can call on which agents to do their bidding (Figure 10-25).

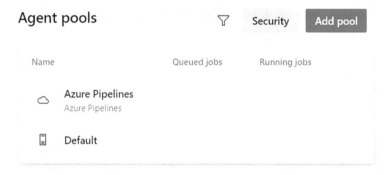

Figure 10-25. *Agent Pool admin*

Agent Pools are a grouping of hosts/environments that share the same setup; if you have builds with different environment requirements, then you will create a pool for each type, for example, Windows and Mac. If one build needs specific software that has limited availability (usually due to licenses), you will then set up a pool for those machines separate from the others, and then another pool for builds that do not need those elements.

The Azure Pipelines is a reference to the Microsoft-hosted agents that your workflows can call upon, while "default" is a free pool to get started with (although I have never used it); to get started, we need to create our own pool specific for our build needs.

To create a new pool, simply click the "**Add Pool**" button in the top right-hand corner of the screen, as shown in Figure 10-26.

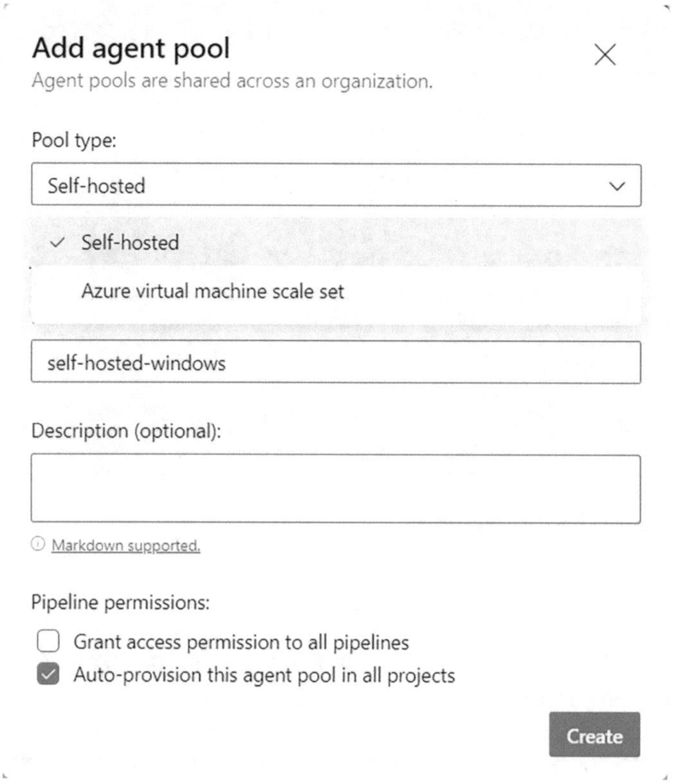

Add agent pool   ✕

Agent pools are shared across an organization.

Pool type:

Self-hosted	⌄

  ✓ Self-hosted

    Azure virtual machine scale set

self-hosted-windows

Description (optional):

ⓘ Markdown supported.

Pipeline permissions:

☐ Grant access permission to all pipelines

☑ Auto-provision this agent pool in all projects

[Create]

Figure 10-26. *Add new Agent Pool*

In the dialog that pops up, select whether this is a self-hosted pool or an Azure pool; in this case, we want to select self-hosted. From there, just give it a friendly name, a description if you like, and choose the Permission options for the pool (which can be changed later).

The "Auto-provision this agent in all projects" option only shows up for Agent Pools created at the organizational level and enables the pool to work for all projects or only specific ones.

With the pool set up, you will see the Pool definition and control screen, which you will end up looking at A LOT in your time with automation, although, at the moment, it is very bare, as you can see in Figure 10-27.

Figure 10-27. *Agent Pool overview*

From here, you can see

- What jobs are running on which hosts, plus the job history of all successes and failures

- The list of agents in this pool (all machines with identical setups) and their current status, like whether they are active, what version of Azure agent they are running, etc.

- Basic details about the pool

- Security setup for the pool, what users can view it and what accounts can access it, etc.

- Analytics details for the performance of agents and concurrency

More importantly, there is the "**NEW AGENT**" button in the top right, which, when clicked, will give us the necessary details for how to set up an agent on your local hardware (Figure 10-28).

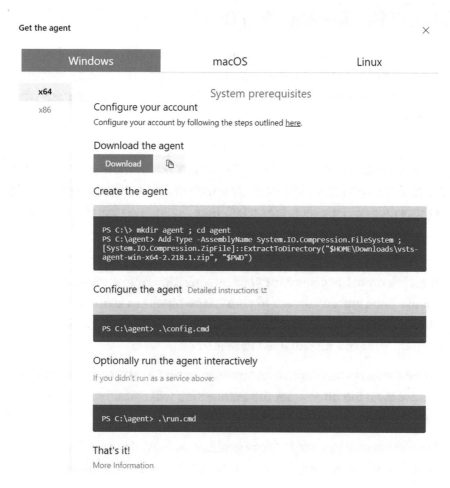

Figure 10-28. *Agent setup*

For this example, I created a pool called **"self-hosted-windows"** to denote the container for all the Windows build hosts that will be self-hosted; this pool name is what you will refer to later when setting up your agent and the pool name you will use in your automation.

If you are setting up a Mac host, then feel free to call it "self-hosted-mac" instead.

The Pools/Groups you set up in the long run will be determined by the types and setups of host you will consume in your automation based on their requirements.

The details are pretty much the same for Windows, Mac, or Linux; download the agent software to the host, run the setup, and off you go. Oh, how I wish it was that simple, but let us continue.

Configuring the Automation User

Most of the instructions/guidance kind of skips over a critical part as it seems almost assumed, but you SHOULD have a dedicated user account for running automation; this has been called out several times in this title, but let us delve more into what it means for Azure Pipelines.

Having a separate account is "optional" but highly recommended, as using personal accounts can cause issues later which could result in you having to set everything up again a second (or third) time, including uninstalling/removing existing agents which is no mean feat.

Whether it is a domain account for your organization or just another Microsoft account that has been granted access to your Azure pipelines is not important, so long as it is a separate account (your company policies if you have them will dictate which you need); ultimately, the account will need access to

- Administrative privileges over the automation host/PC; this includes access to all the directories the automation will use, as well as the registry and other admin tasks.

- Pipeline access to your Azure organization, as well as granular permissions to the projects the automation will need to run against.

- Unity/API access to any external resources needed.

Permissions are granted via Permissions groups at both the organization and project levels via the "**PERMISSIONS**" tab in the **SETTINGS**, which looks like Figure 10-29.

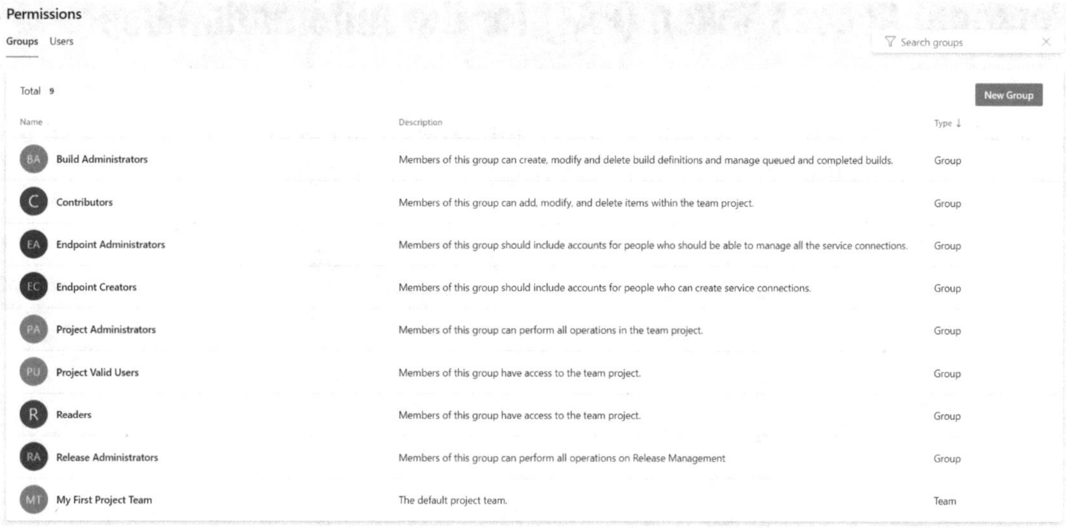

Figure 10-29. *Pipeline Permissions*

Each group then has specific access to all or part of the Azure DevOps setup. There is too much to go through for this title, and you can read more about what each of these groups does and the access they give here:

```
https://learn.microsoft.com/en-us/azure/devops/pipelines/security/resour
ces?view=azure-devops
```

Suffice to say, the user you define to run your automation should have access to the **"Project Administrators"** group, whether that is your own account or the dedicated account for the automation.

Personal Access Token (PAT) for the Automation User

Additionally, you will need to create a Personal Access Token (**PAT**) for the user by clicking the "**User Settings**" icon in the top right-hand corner of the screen next to your user icon and selecting "Personal Access Tokens" (Figure 10-30).

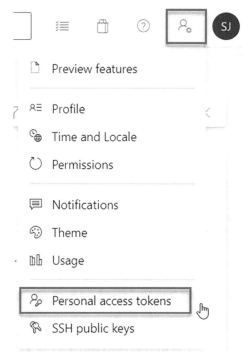

Figure 10-30. *Personal Access Token view*

From here, you can create a new PAT which you will use in setting up the agent; this will be used to grant specific permission to the user from the automation agent (Figure 10-31).

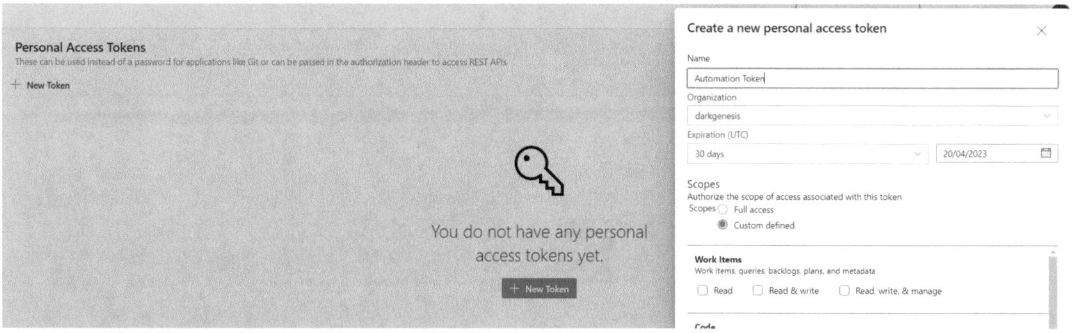

Figure 10-31. *Personal Access Token setup*

Which permissions you select IS important; at a minimum, it needs the "**Agent Pools (read, manage)**" scope. For more details, check out the Agent setup guide section on permissions:

https://learn.microsoft.com/en-us/azure/devops/pipelines/agents/v2-windows?view=azure-devops#authenticate-with-a-personal-access-token-pat

---

In my experience, I have always used the "Full Access" mode for the automation agent as it is a secure account/access. This has saved me from many headaches in operating automation agents. However, it will be up to you to decide how "locked down" the automation account needs to be and resolve the issues while setting up access.

Once created, you will get a prompt to show you the generated token, but **BEWARE**, this is the ONE and ONLY time you will see this token; you can never see it again once generated (Figure 10-32).

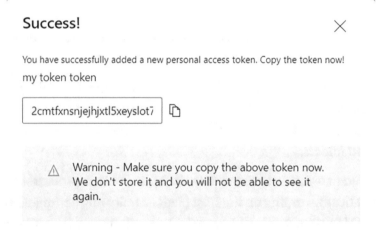

Figure 10-32. *Personal Access Token key*

Make a copy of the token in a SECURE place and store it for use later. If you lose it, you will have to generate a new one!

Mac Users and Build Hosts

A small note/section for users creating Mac agents on a "spare 🏚" Apple Mac they have lying around to do iOS automation. This has caused me endless amounts of fun for the additional limitations placed on Apple developers to get their projects built.

On a Mac, the automation runs as the currently logged-on user; there is no such thing as a background user/account (that I am aware of); even running the automation as a "service" requires the user that installed the service to be logged on for the automation agent to even start, and that user MUST remain logged on for automation to run.

If the automation user is NOT logged on, the automation agent **WILL NOT RUN**.

Effectively, Mac build hosts are dedicated machines (unlike Windows) and can only be used for automation.

When setting up a Mac, ensure

- The automation user is logged on; if restarted, this user will need to be logged on again or set up to automatically log on.

- The automation user needs SPECIFIC access to files and folders on the host; just being an admin is not enough; you may need to check folder permissions to ensure they have read and write access to all required folders.

- You need to override the Mac default ability to block processes from automatically running on the host (see the following command) or MANUALLY allow each and every DLL required to run automation on the Mac.

- The Mac user will also need access to an Apple developer account which has access to the Apple organization. Thankfully though, this does not need to be separate and can be any valid Apple developer account.

- The Unity installation needs to be set up and registered for building Apple apps. Just run a few end-to-end tests building an app and PUBLISHING to TestFlight. This will save you HOURS of head scratching later.

I found the following command which can enable "Allow apps downloaded from Anywhere":

sudo spctl --master-disable

Source: `https://github.com/microsoft/azure-pipelines-agent/issues/2457`

I wish you well on your journey to retain your hair while getting automation running on a Mac.

Make sure to also check out the "unity-ci-cd-ios" channel on the "Unity DevOps discord server": `https://discord.gg/ntkWUu6A`.

Configuring the Host

With everything in place, it is time for the final showdown, to get the Azure agent installed on a machine ready to accept requests.

The critical information you will require to enter this section is

- The name for your agent; remember you will likely need more than one eventually, so NUMBER them (much easier than code names).

- The "Server URL" to your DevOps organization:
  https://dev.azure.com/<your org>

If you are registering it for a single project, then this URL will also include the project name, for example, *https://dev.azure.com/*<your org>/<your project>, copied from the browser in cases where there is any HTML encoding for the URL (%20% instead of space).

- The PAT (Personal Access Token) to access the Azure DevOps organization you created earlier.

- The Agent Pool name you wish to install for. The name of the pool you created earlier, for example, "**self-hosted-windows**".

Fear not, you will likely take SEVERAL attempts to get the agent installed; I know I do almost every time I need to set up a new agent, just because…

Provided you have all the required software installed, such as:

- Your chosen operating system (I will be using Windows for the example).

- **Unity**, obviously.

- The Unity modules for the platforms you want to build for, including any dependencies such as the Android SDK/NDK. (These can be installed through automation, but save yourself time in the beginning.)

- PowerShell or Bash, based on the scripting language you are using in your pipeline. In this case, install PowerShell by default:

  ```
  https://learn.microsoft.com/en-us/powershell/scripting/
  install/installing-powershell-on-windows?view=powershell-7.3
  ```

- The Git command-line client (because automation does not use UI); for Windows, it is

  ```
  https://gitforwindows.org/
  ```

- Visual Studio to run your build; Visual Studio Community edition is sufficient in most cases.

Plus, any other software/packages needed to build/run your project.

Before you start, you should clone your project locally; open it up and perform a manual build for your target platform(s), "just in case," as you may have forgotten something. Before we install the agent, you want to ensure there are no other obvious issues in producing builds.

With that ready, assuming you have downloaded the client to the machine, let us begin:

1. Create a folder at the ROOT of the drive that will host the automation. Having it at the root of the drive reduces the risk of any long folder names generated in builds and can cause issues. (On a Mac, you might want to use the automation user's "documentation" folder instead due to permissions; just use your best path.)

2. Name the folder using a single letter (again, to keep the path short); I use "A" for simplicity (A = Azure).

3. In the "A" folder, create a unique folder for your agent. You can skip this if you are only planning on running a single agent on the host, but I always like to plan ahead, just in case.

4. Name the agent folder "01", or "*agent-01*", keeping it short.

5. Unzip the contents of the Agent download into the "agent" folder; it should then contain the agent zip contents and not another folder.

6. Open a command prompt window (**with administrative privileges**, unless it is a Mac, as SUDO is not allowed) or terminal window on a Mac and navigate to the "agent" folder.

7. Start the process by running "config.cmd" on Windows or "./config.sh" in the case of a Mac.

Now the real fun begins.

---

8. You will be prompted for the "**server url**," so paste or type the "Server URL" you recorded earlier.

9. You will then be asked for the **authentication type**; just hit **Enter** here to accept the default, PAT authentication.

10. Now paste or type in your **PAT** token you recorded earlier.

11. Next, you will need to enter the Agent Pool your agent will be registered under. You can hit enter to use the default, but I find it best to set up the pools yourself, so you understand what is registered where, so type "self-hosted-windows" (or "self-hosted-mac" if you created a Mac pool) or whatever the name of the pool you created was.

12. With the pool created, you simply then need to give the agent a name. Save yourself a lot of headaches and keep the folder name and the name of the agent the same; this will make it easier to manage going forward. Name the agent "**agent-01**" as that was the name of the folder containing the agent in this example.

13. Finally, we need to set the folder name that will be used for all work done by the agent, where code is cloned to, logs generated, and builds run. In keeping with the idea that we want to keep the path short, name this folder "**w**" or just hit enter to select the default "_work".

With the agent created, you then need to decide whether you will run the agent manually or automatically, and this is where the path differs on Windows as opposed to Mac or Linux.

Windows

For Windows, you will be prompted whether you want to run the agent as a service or not; if you select "Y," it will prompt you for the administrative account you want the service to be run under and its password. This will then create a new background service for the agent which will start automatically when the host starts. You can either accept the default (which to be honest I usually do) or select a specific account, such as the automation user account that you set up; the choice is up to you.

Mac/Linux

For Mac and Linux, the service will not be installed automatically; you have to do this manually using the "./svc.sh" script which is pretty automatic; however, on Mac at least (I have not personally installed it on Linux, unless you count Mac), the story does not end there, as although the service is registered, you need to enable the script to be able to run. Either you will need to go to the Apple Preferences ➤ Security window and enable each and every DLL to run (I did it once being ignorant of Mac operation; it was not fun) or run the SUDO command mentioned earlier in the agent folder to ignore security for the scripts in the agent folder.

Either way, you should ask your respective Mac person to help, or do as I have done, which is again up to you.

Agent Completion

If you have typed everything in correctly, not missed any spaces, selected the right accounts, and done all the bits, you should have a command prompt result similar to the one shown in Figure 10-33.

```
C:\a\agent-01>dir
 Volume in drive C has no label.
 Volume Serial Number is B413-5102

 Directory of C:\a\agent-01

21/03/2023  13:11    <DIR>          .
21/03/2023  13:06    <DIR>          ..
21/03/2023  13:07    <DIR>          bin
21/03/2023  13:06             2,967 config.cmd
21/03/2023  13:07    <DIR>          externals
21/03/2023  13:06             3,190 run.cmd
21/03/2023  13:08    <DIR>          _diag
               2 File(s)          6,157 bytes
               5 Dir(s)  231,058,460,672 bytes free

C:\a\agent-01>config.cmd

          ___        _____ _            _ _
         /   \___  _|  ____(_)          | (_)
        / /\ / _ \| | |__   _ _ __   ___| |_ _ __   ___  ___
       / /_//_/\_\| |  __| | | '_ \ / _ \ | | '_ \ / _ \/ __|
      /___,'     \_| |    | | | |_) |  __/ | | | | |  __/\__ \
                      |_|    |_| .__/ \___|_|_|_| |_|\___||___/
                               | |
          agent v2.218.1       |_|        (commit f52b8ff)


>> Connect:

Enter server URL > https://dev.azure.com/darkgenesis
Enter authentication type (press enter for PAT) >
Enter personal access token > **************************************************
Connecting to server ...

>> Register Agent:

Enter agent pool (press enter for default) > self-hosted-windows
Enter agent name (press enter for DESKTOP-M5Q1ID0) > agent-01
Scanning for tool capabilities.
Connecting to the server.
Successfully added the agent
Testing agent connection.
Enter work folder (press enter for _work) > w
2023-03-21 13:23:05Z: Settings Saved.
Enter run agent as service? (Y/N) (press enter for N) > y
Enter enable SERVICE_SID_TYPE_UNRESTRICTED for agent service (Y/N) (press enter for N) > y
Enter User account to use for the service (press enter for NT AUTHORITY\NETWORK SERVICE) >
Granting file permissions to 'NT AUTHORITY\NETWORK SERVICE'.
Service vstsagent.darkgenesis.self-hosted-windows.agent-01 successfully installed
Service vstsagent.darkgenesis.self-hosted-windows.agent-01 successfully set recovery option
Service vstsagent.darkgenesis.self-hosted-windows.agent-01 successfully set to delayed auto start
Service vstsagent.darkgenesis.self-hosted-windows.agent-01 successfully set SID type
Service vstsagent.darkgenesis.self-hosted-windows.agent-01 successfully configured
Enter whether to prevent service starting immediately after configuration is finished? (Y/N) (press enter for N) >
Service vstsagent.darkgenesis.self-hosted-windows.agent-01 started successfully
```

Figure 10-33. *Windows agent installation result*

Fear ye not, many slip-ups can happen while installing the agent; if you can cancel with "Ctrl+C" or "Cmd+Z" before you reach the point of "Successfully added agent," then you can simply restart again. If you pass this point however, you will need to uninstall the current agent before starting again using the following command:

./config.cmd remove

or on a Mac:

./config.sh remove

which will uninstall the agent from the host and deregister it from Azure. You will need your PAT to update Azure or remove it manually from the UI. Make sure you want to, as the remove command does not ask you if you want to, it just DOES IT!

With the agent installed, you can check the Azure DevOps management interface for your selected Agent Pool and see your new agent in all its glory up and running (hopefully), as in Figure 10-34.

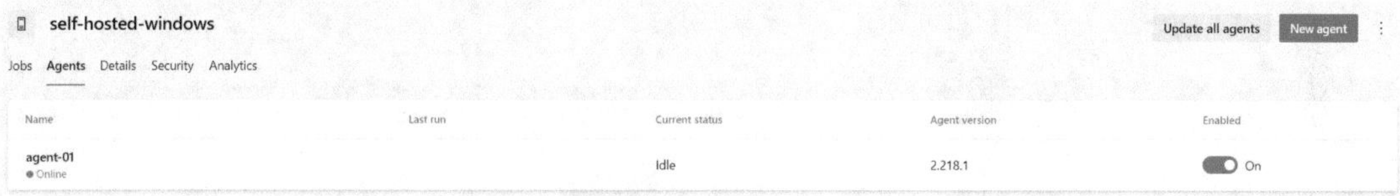

Figure 10-34. *Agent Pool – Agent view*

Returning to Your Agent Configuration

The final step in this long journey is to test out our new self-hosted agent. We can do this by simply changing the "**Pool**" definition in our YAML configuration.

In the example repository, I have created a separate "***azure-pipelines-self-hosted.yml***" file for comparison; if you use separate Pipeline yml definitions, you will need additional Pipelines set up in the Azure DevOps interface.

```
pool:
  name: self-hosted-windows
```

Now instead of using the expensive Microsoft hosting for the intensive task of building and publishing our Unity project, we can use our much reasonably priced hardware situated at our desk. Run the pipeline again after making the change in the YAML editor and give it a try (Figure 10-35).

Figure 10-35.   *Workflow now running on my PC*

Summary

Now your eyes have been opened to the world of professional automation and the opportunities it gives (as well as potentially saving you money), the world is yours to experiment with and explore.

A few things you can try out:

- Try building several builds in the same pipeline, or better yet, create several pipelines to make concurrent builds (provided you have enough agents to take on the task; in one project, I have six agents to run multiple builds at once on a single machine).

- Explore the rest of the Azure Marketplace and the many integrations available, so much choice.

- Check out Apple integration using the Marketplace Apple plugins – although personally, I use manual Xcode scripts to do my builds.

- Play with AppCenter integration and deploy your builds through AppCenter automatically.

The world is yours, but I am sure you did find there was a lot of work involved in setting up Azure integration, primarily because Azure is an enterprise-focused automation pathway (although it is still my preference for producing an actual build). So let us next look into the world of GitHub Actions which most consider as the lightweight successor to Azure pipelines.

CHAPTER 11

Setting Up GitHub Actions

Originally, GitHub was just about source control, a safe and decentralized offering to host your code for free (if it was public and open source). When Microsoft bought GitHub, things started to evolve and grow; one of the biggest areas of growth was in automation. From that date, Microsoft saw an opportunity to learn from how they evolved their original Azure Pipelines automation and start afresh with those learnings, eventually growing GitHub Actions into a competing product with their own services. You might ask why they would do this, but ultimately it was in their own self-interest; Azure while powerful can be cumbersome; GitHub is new, fresh, easier to use, and more available.

To date, this evolution continues with more and more Azure Pipelines features being rolled into GitHub Actions, as well as new community-led features being introduced, and it does not stop there. Best of all, GitHub continues to offer free services to all (part of why the Azure offering is also free). The latest enhancements are also AI led, with new code protection and scanning services aimed to make your own code safer and alert you to unsafe practices in your own code before it starts to cause issues in the wild; this is crucial as attacks are becoming more intense, and the ways that malicious entities use to try and subvert seemingly harmless functionality are getting more and more technical. Microsoft truly is trying to help reduce exposure through its own learnings and discoveries to make coding itself a secure first approach, even if you are not 100% aware of the new risks out there.

Let us dig in.

© Simon Jackson 2023
S. Jackson, *Accelerating Unity Through Automation*, https://doi.org/10.1007/978-1-4842-9508-3_11

Prerequisites

To get started with GitHub Actions, you do not need much:

1. A GitHub account (I would also recommend setting up an additional separate account to run the automation as well)

2. Your choice of source control repository, which can also be on Azure if you wish.

3. A Unity project in the repository

1. GitHub Account

Unlike Azure, any GitHub account will do; from here, you can set up whatever organizations or additional accounts you require. Your personal account will not interfere with whatever you also have access to or contribute to; it is more of a single identity used for promoting your works and security for your identity.

If you have not seen it of late, I would just create a new GitHub account for fun (although better if you are doing it for your separate automation account); the process is fun, and GitHub has basically gamified it in the style of the 1980s hacking movies ☺.

I also highly recommend setting up an **ADDITIONAL GITHUB ACCOUNT** which will be used by the automation; this ensures it is secure, and any private keys required for the automation are owned and managed by this account (Personal Access Tokens often get invalidated with personal accounts and can wreak havoc with automation). It keeps things separate and clean to avoid risk and confusion. The automation account should also have its own access to the source control for the project (e.g., a GitHub account) to maintain the separation. Keep the account secure, enable 2FA (which you should have on everything anyway), and a random secure password (locked away for safekeeping), exactly the same as Azure.

This account is effectively going to be running your automation business for you, so keep it safe!

2. Source Control

GitHub actions are primarily defined for use with GitHub repositories, which is where the automation lives and runs; it really does not have a need to work elsewhere. Like its competitors who all have their own offerings, GitHub automation is run from and enacted from GitHub repositories.

You can, however, connect to practically anything else through script within your automation if you need to download/clone or use other resources; there are no limitations to speak of, but the automation will only run from GitHub whether it is through a schedule or via events that happen in the GitHub API.

3. You Need a Unity Project

Ideally, the Unity project should be hosted inside the GitHub repository, but as mentioned earlier, it does not have to (only the automation itself **MUST** be), but in all honesty, if you are using GitHub automation, it does not make too much sense to then put the code elsewhere. However, it is worth mentioning how you should make your project available; you can either

- Put your project in the root of your repository – which works fine with most source control "ignore files" to omit Unity's background folders like the Library, Temp, and Build folders.

- (Recommended) Put your project in a folder within the repository – Unity also supports building from a subfolder in your source control project, which is sometimes preferred by developers as it keeps the Unity parts of your project away from the source control files like ReadMes, git files, and such.

Just make sure the default Unity git ignore files are not targeting the ROOT of your source control folder, else you may end up with the extremely large and unneeded Library folder checked into source control, which makes downloading the project VERY long and will cost you pennies in your Unity Cloud Build; time is money!

Know the Costs

GitHub is a LOT more transparent regarding the costs for their automation services; these are highlighted in the primary cost breakdown (Figure 11-1) for your individual/organizational GitHub accounts, with 2000 minutes per month of free hosted agent time, 200 more minutes than Azure.

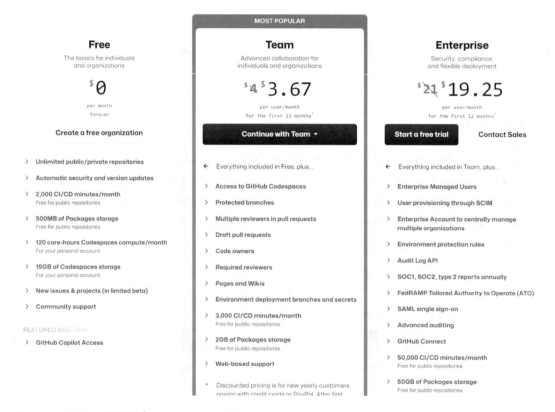

Figure 11-1. *GitHub account pricing*

Where Git differs is that they also give a better breakdown of what these minutes mean when using their services in their prices (anyone who has tried to use the Azure pricing calculator will know what I mean), as shown in Figure 11-2.

Product	Storage	Minutes (per month)
GitHub Free	500 MB	2,000
GitHub Pro	1 GB	3,000
GitHub Free for organizations	500 MB	2,000
GitHub Team	2 GB	3,000
GitHub Enterprise Cloud	50 GB	50,000

Jobs that run on Windows and macOS runners that GitHub hosts consume minutes at 2 and 10 times the rate that jobs on Linux runners consume. For example, using 1,000 Windows minutes would consume 2,000 of the minutes included in your account. Using 1,000 macOS minutes, would consume 10,000 minutes included in your account.

Minute multipliers 🔗

Operating system	Minute multiplier
Linux	1
Windows	2
macOS	10

Figure 11-2. *GitHub pricing breakdown*

The Linux runtime is obviously the cheapest, with Windows a little more expensive and Mac being a LOT more expensive overall (have you seen the price of Macs these days?). For more details on GitHub's pricing structure for automation, check their billing page here:

```
https://docs.github.com/en/billing/managing-billing-for-github-actions/
about-billing-for-github-actions
```

Supported Platforms

Like Azure, GitHub itself does not limit building for any Unity platform; all you need is the server requirements to build it (whatever Unity supports through its editor) and the pipeline configuration to run it:

- iOS

- Android

- Windows desktop

- Windows UWP

- Mac OS desktop

- Linux desktop

- WebGL

- Xbox

- PlayStation

- Nintendo Switch (although there are several caveats)

- A new platform just released that Unity suddenly supports months later

Ultimately, there are no limitations; if you can build it on your Windows/Mac/Linux desktop, then you can build it in the cloud or on your desktop as a self-hosted agent.

Getting Started – Make a Project

After the wholly Unity-owned land of UGS and the extensive setup and management you must sift through with Azure Pipelines, GitHub Actions will feel like a breath of fresh air, because to get set up with GitHub actions, you do not need anything; in fact, you already have what you need with an existing GitHub repository.

As previously stated, GitHub Actions are limited only in that they require a GitHub repository to work from, although in fairness that is not where your code needs to be (you can host it in another Git repository), but in reality, why would you complicate the process by putting things in different places?

Once you have a GitHub repository with your project in it, you are already 90% of the way there, with the last 10% deciding where and how you want to automate your project (although we all know the costs of that last 10%, don't we?).

GitHub Actions Permissions and Configuration

GitHub provides some overarching configuration for maintaining access to GitHub actions behaviors, which can be viewed by going to either

- "**Project ➤ Settings ➤ Actions ➤ General**" for per-project Actions settings

- "**Organization ➤ Settings ➤ Actions ➤ General**" for organizational configuration

See Figure 11-3.

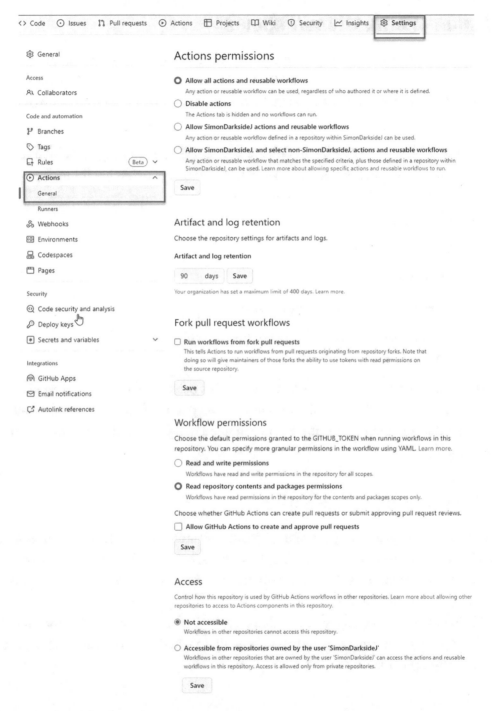

Figure 11-3. *GitHub Actions settings*

These configurations break down into the following groups.

1. Actions Permissions/Policies

The Permissions/Policies simply determine which actions are allowed, mainly to protect the repositories from anyone updating the workflows and including GitHub Actions that are not in the best interest of the project. By default, this is set to "**ALLOW ALL ACTIONS**."

When your project is forked by an outside collaborator, Actions are disabled by default, but can be enabled by the collaborator unless you disable them.

The options range from

- Allow All

- Disable Actions

- Allow only those created by the owner

- Allow those created by the owner and a configured list of "allowed" actions

Which option you select is up to you, but if it is a private repository managed only by you, simply set it to all as you already control everything. If you are managing all the repositories for your organization, you will need to decide on the level of control required.

2. Artifact and Log Retention

The retention dates are simply how long GitHub will store any published log or artifact generated from the workflows, such as build reports, build artifacts, and so on. The more you keep/store, the more likely you will breach the "free" tier allowance and end up being charged for storage.

The default is 90 days, so if you are doing a lot of builds and publishing the logs, then you will want to review this; how long you keep them will depend on how useful past logs are for future work.

3. Fork or Pull Request from Outside Collaborators

Simply put, you can enforce that you must approve any execution of your workflows from Forks of your project. Forks will still need their own agent setup, and it will use their time/resources for any hosted agents, not yours.

For organizations, you can also set control for private repositories, which is turned OFF by default in case you are having issues!

4. Workflow Permissions

By default, any activity through automation is read-only set in the workflow permissions using the GITHUB_TOKEN of the user running the automation; this ensures that nothing can update your repository through automation even if their access allows them to; this can only be overridden with a PAT that has improved permissions. If you have workflows which need to "push" to the repository, you will need to review this.

To read more about the workflow permissions, check the Microsoft documentation on controlling GITHUB_TOKEN permissions here:

```
https://docs.github.com/en/actions/security-guides/automatic-
token-authentication#modifying-the-permissions-for-the-
GitHub_token
```

---

5. Required Workflows (Organization Only)

At the organizational level, you can set MANDATORY workflows that must be run by all repositories within the organization; this can range from logging actions that report use/execution to code validation/qualification actions that ensure a minimum level of quality from any activity. Microsoft makes great use of this feature for all its public repositories to ensure all contributors meet a minimum level of security (2FA, GitHub agreements) and that certain checks are always carried out.

Personal Access Token (PAT) for the Automation User

Access to your repositories through automation requires an automation user and a secure access key called a Personal Access Token (PAT for short); this is a secure key to do specific tasks without needing to log in.

You do not "have" to create a separate account for the automated user, but it is "highly recommended"; also, the GitHub new account creation process is kinda fun, so you should try it out.

With the user that will generate the token logged in, you will need to navigate to the Settings for the user by clicking the arrow next to the username in the top right-hand corner of the screen and selecting "Settings," as shown in Figure 11-4.

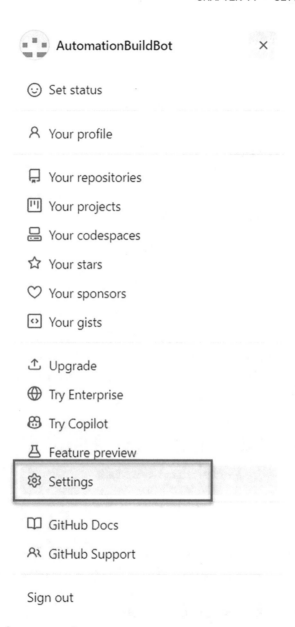

Figure 11-4. *GitHub user settings*

Next, you will need to select "**Developer settings**" on the left-hand side of the screen, right down at the bottom, to access the secure token configuration, as shown in Figure 11-5.

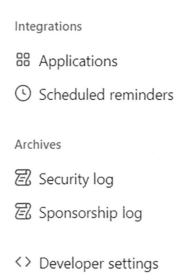

Figure 11-5. *Developer settings selection*

Finally, from here you can create a new PAT which you will use in setting up the agent; this can be either a "classic" token or one of the newer "fine-grained" style tokens; for simplicity, let us create a "**CLASSIC**" token (Figure 11-6).

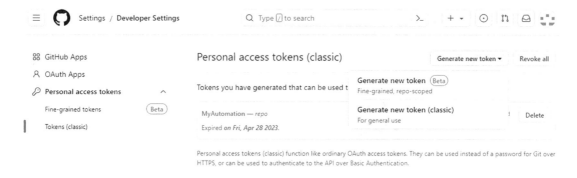

Figure 11-6. *Personal Access Token creation*

For more details on the differences between the "classic" and the newer "fine-grained" tokens, you can read about them from GitHub here:

https://docs.github.com/en/authentication/keeping-your-account-and-data-secure/managing-your-personal-access-tokens

---

When you are creating the token, which permissions you select IS important; at a minimum, it needs the "repo" scope. For more details, check out the GitHub Scopes for OAuth apps guide on permissions (Figure 11-7):

```
https://docs.g'ithub.com/en/apps/oauth-apps/building-oauth-apps/scopes-
for-oauth-apps
```

New personal access token (classic)

Personal access tokens (classic) function like ordinary OAuth access tokens. They can be used instead of a password for Git over HTTPS, or can be used to authenticate to the API over Basic Authentication.

Note

> MyAutomation

What's this token for?

Expiration *

> 30 days   ⇕   The token will expire on Thu, Jul 20 2023

Select scopes

Scopes define the access for personal tokens. Read more about OAuth scopes.

☑ **repo**	Full control of private repositories
☑ repo:status	Access commit status
☑ repo_deployment	Access deployment status
☑ public_repo	Access public repositories
☑ repo:invite	Access repository invitations
☑ security_events	Read and write security events
☐ **workflow**	Update GitHub Action workflows
☐ **write:packages**	Upload packages to GitHub Package Registry
☐ read:packages	Download packages from GitHub Package Registry

Figure 11-7. *Personal Access Token setup*

The "**EXPIRATION**" of the token is also something you will need to consider as it is something you will need to manage manually. The best security advice is to have a token expire within a given period and then generate a new key and update your pipeline, although if you choose to, you can set the expiry to "Never Expire" and only change it when you need/want to. Which path you choose is yours to make.

Once created, you will get a prompt to show you the generated token (Figure 11-8), but BEWARE, this is the ONE and ONLY time you will see this token; you can never see it again once generated. Make a copy of the token in a SECURE place and store it for use later. If you lose it, you will have to generate a new one!

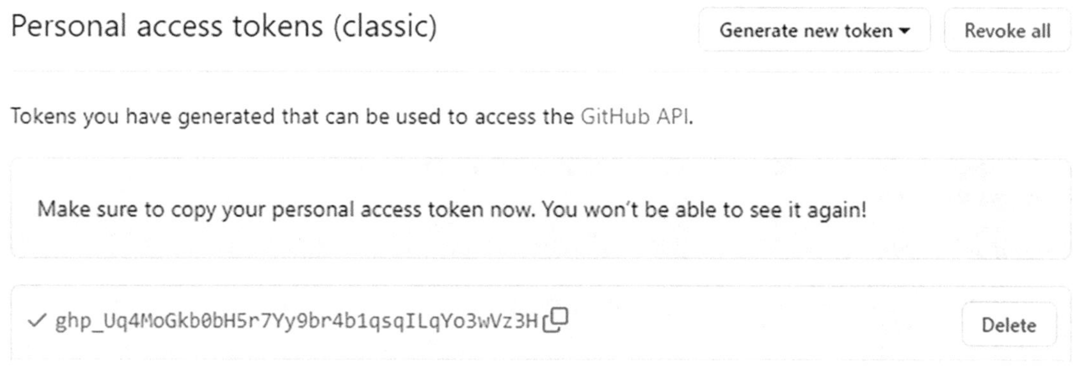

Personal access tokens (classic)   Generate new token ▾   Revoke all

Tokens you have generated that can be used to access the GitHub API.

Make sure to copy your personal access token now. You won't be able to see it again!

✓ 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 ⎘   Delete

Figure 11-8. *Personal Access Token key*

GitHub Actions Marketplace

GitHub provides a whole community-driven marketplace for all the different Actions available for use in automation on GitHub; there are tens of thousands of freely available Actions for use; granted, not all of them will actually be useful (especially for Unity), and there may be many duplicates as they are all community sponsored, but there are many great options out there, as shown in Figure 11-9.

You can find the marketplace at `https://github.com/marketplace?type=actions`.

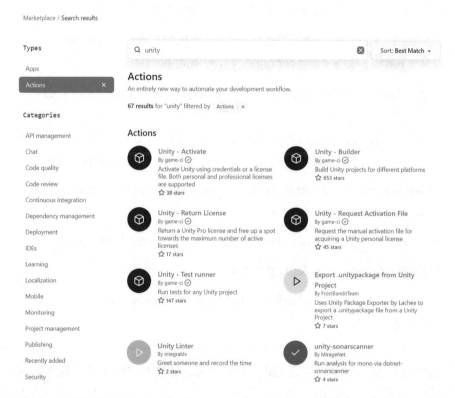

Figure 11-9. *GitHub Actions Marketplace*

Like many other community-led source of public offerings, look through what is available, read the reviews, and check it before using it in any production environment. But also check for alternates as some developers clone other Actions and apply subtle improvements; the best do PRs back to the original, but not all PRs are accepted, and some developers just want to do what they think is best. It is a bit "wild west" out there, but there are many good packages to find.

Using the GameCI Actions to Automate Unity Tasks

One of the best public actions for building and testing Unity projects is the GameCI actions, which you can read more about here:

    https://game.ci/

You do not HAVE to use GameCI's actions, and you "can" build it yourself, but it can become tricky and complex; sometimes, it is just easier to "stand on the shoulders of giants" (as we did in Azure with Dino's UnityDevOps package).

If you want to see what the scripting requirements are like for building it yourself, check out the Reality Collective repository for reusable actions:

    https://github.com/realitycollective/reusableworkflows

GameCI offers several pre-built GitHub actions (which we will be using in this title) to perform the required tasks for dealing with Unity in automation, such as

- Unity Activation – If you need to build using a Pro License. Required if you are building on hosted agents

- Test Runner – To execute and report on tests in your Unity project

- Builder – Builds your Unity project

- Deploy – Enables automatic deployment to Google Play, Apple App Store, or Steam

---

GameCI also natively supports GitLab and CircleCI if you choose to; however, we are focusing on GitHub Actions in this title.

A good feature that GameCI also recommends for when using hosted agents is to cache the "Library" folder that Unity generates to save some time when opening the project for Test/Build, although this assumes you are always using the same version of Unity for each run; if you update Unity, you will still incur the additional time in a build to regenerate the "Library" folder.

Setting Up a GameCI Actions Workflow

As you already have a GitHub repository, you have everything you need to get started with your first workflow; to begin, we simply need to set up the folder structure and then create your first workflow definition on GitHub.

Using GitHub, we do not even need to clone the project; you can edit the repository online thanks to GitHub and Microsoft's investment into VSCode online which can be accessed either from

- Hitting "." on the keyboard either in branch view or while looking at a PR (which opens a PR-specific view showing just the changes in that PR)

- Changing the URL from "GitHub.com" to "GitHub.dev"

Entering the VSCode web view, you get to see everything in your repository, ready and waiting to use (almost as if you were on your desktop) straight from your browser (Figure 11-10).

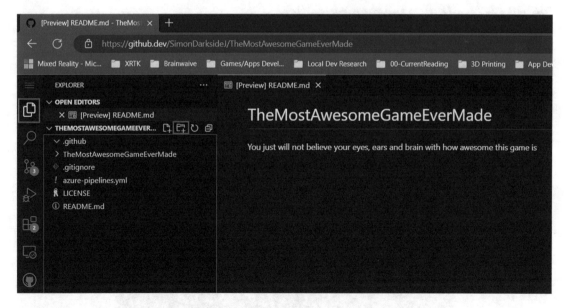

Figure 11-10. *VSCode web view from GitHub*

GitHub actions need some folders set up to get up and running; first, create a ".GITHUB" folder to host all GitHub-related configuration and files, then create a "WORKFLOWS" to hold all your workflow configuration that GitHub will monitor as your repository grows and changes:

.GitHub
➤ *workflows*

To create a folder, simply switch to file view using the document icon in the top left (which is the default view) and then click the second "ADD FOLDER" icon next to the name of the repository, as shown in Figure 11-11.

Figure 11-11. *Adding the required folders*

Once you have created the ".GitHub" and "workflows" folders, you can then use the adjacent "New File" button to add your workflow YAML file and create a "PIPELINE-GAMECI.YML" file, as shown in Figure 11-12.

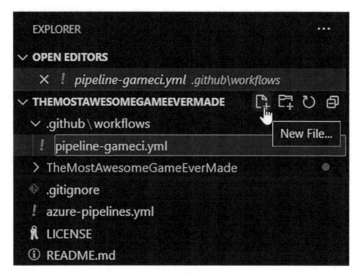

Figure 11-12. *Adding new workflow YAML*

VSCode will automatically open the new file, or you can select it in the tree view on the left-hand side; simply replace the contents with the following, and we will then walk through the configuration:

```yaml
name: GitHub Actions example using GameCI

on:
  workflow_dispatch:

jobs:
  build:
    name: Build my project
    runs-on: ubuntu-latest
    steps:
      # Checkout
      - name: Checkout repository
        uses: actions/checkout@v3

      # Cache
      - uses: actions/cache@v2
        with:
          path: TheMostAwesomeGameEverMade/Library
          key: Library-${{ hashFiles('Assets/**', 'Packages/**',
          'ProjectSettings/**') }}
          restore-keys: |
            Library-

      # Build
      - name: Build project
        uses: game-ci/unity-builder@v2
        env:
          UNITY_LICENSE: ${{ secrets.UNITY_LICENSE }}
          UNITY_EMAIL: ${{ secrets.UNITY_EMAIL }}
          UNITY_PASSWORD: ${{ secrets.UNITY_PASSWORD }}
        with:
          projectPath: TheMostAwesomeGameEverMade
          targetPlatform: WebGL
```

```
# Output
- uses: actions/upload-artifact@v2
  with:
    name: Build
    path: TheMostAwesomeGameEverMade/build
```

You will note a major difference between GitHub Actions and Azure Pipelines use of external workflows in that you do not need to install anything. You simply need to ensure the automation account has access to the external workflow/action (most are public); no preinstall is required.

The workflow (built from the GameCI Actions examples) has the following steps:

1. Checkout – When the automation starts, get a copy of the repository from the branch it was run from.

2. Cache Library – If the pipeline was previously run, copy the "Library" folder from the cache to speed up load and build times. The cache is updated when the workflow finishes.

Note you may want to override this if your Unity version changes or packages are removed, same as you would do locally to clear out your Library folder.

---

3. Build Project – Uses the GameCI action to start a Unity image using the version of Unity as identified within the project and specifying which platform to build for.

GameCI requires Unity to be activated in order for builds to run; this includes both Personal and Professional editions. Check the following section for activating Personal licenses, which is a bit involved.

---

4. Output Build – Publish the output of the build to the GitHub
    Actions publish area, which will show up in the summary for the
    workflow run on GitHub.

The workflow is currently configured for MANUAL execution for testing; in reality,
you would have the workflow activate on a pull request or push to the repository.

With the workflow setup, there are a few prerequisite steps to make the workflow
operate correctly, namely:

- License Activation

- Configuring Secrets

License Activation with GameCI

As stated previously, GameCI requires Unity to be activated in order to run, both Personal and Pro editions.

If you are using Unity Pro, you only need to specify your Unity License Number when running the pipeline and you are done; see the GameCI documentation for more information:

```
https://game.ci/docs/GitHub/activation#professional-license
```

Note   The workflow described earlier assumes you are using Unity Personal; if you are using Pro, you will need to change the "UNITY_LICENSE" argument with a "UNITY_SERIAL" argument.

For Unity Personal, the licensing is a bit more involved, the process looking something like this:

1. Create a separate GitHub Actions workflow to generate a Unity "license request."

2. Upload the license request to Unity while signed in to your Unity account and download the "License Activation" file.

3. Open the License Activation file and copy the contents into a Secret parameter on GitHub (as you do not want to publish your license) – see the next section.

Full details, steps, and configuration are documented here on GameCI's site:

```
https://game.ci/docs/GitHub/activation#personal-license
```

Creating Secrets on GitHub for the Project

As you do not want to share your keys, usernames, and password, GitHub (like Azure) provides you with a mechanism to store these outside of your workflow in such a way that even you cannot read them after they are saved; this is done from the Repository Settings view under "**SECRETS AND VARIABLES ➤ ACTIONS**" (Figure 11-13).

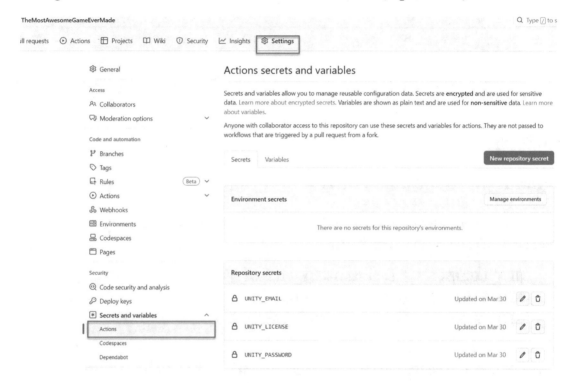

Figure 11-13. *GitHub Actions Secrets*

From here, you can simply click "**NEW REPOSITORY SECRET**"; give the secret a name and then the value that will be returned in that secret (Figure 11-14).

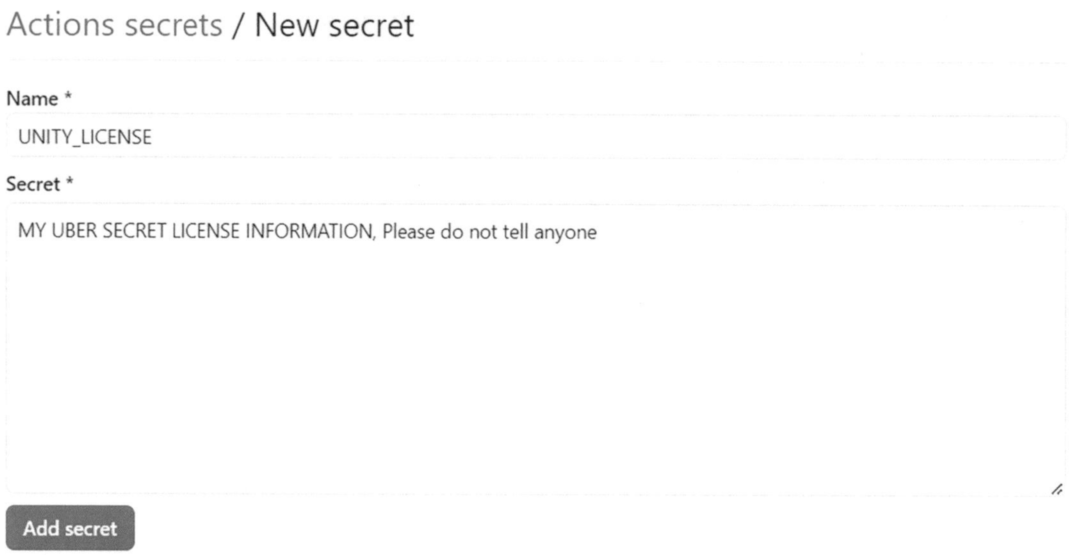

Actions secrets / New secret

Name *

UNITY_LICENSE

Secret *

MY UBER SECRET LICENSE INFORMATION, Please do not tell anyone

Add secret

Figure 11-14. *New repository secret*

These secrets can then be accessed in the workflow by specifying the keyword "**SECRET**" followed by the secret's name:

```
UNITY_LICENSE: ${{ secrets.UNITY_LICENSE }}
UNITY_EMAIL: ${{ secrets.UNITY_EMAIL }}
UNITY_PASSWORD: ${{ secrets.UNITY_PASSWORD }}
```

Secrets can also be registered at the organization level if you wish instead of per project; see the documentation here for more information:

```
https://docs.github.com/en/actions/security-guides/encrypted-
secrets#creating-encrypted-secrets-for-an-organization
```

As required, create the three preceding secrets (they are CASE SENSITIVE) and enter the respective values for your account as the values. For the license, make sure to paste in the "License Activation" file contents and NOT the license request as it will not work!

Also, remember if it is a Pro license, use "**UNITY_SERIAL**" instead of License and set your Unity serial as the value.

Running the Workflow

With the "**Pipeline-gameci.yml**" configured and the secrets registered, you can now switch to the "**Actions**" tab in your repository, and assuming there are no errors with your workflow file, you should see what is shown in Figure 11-15.

Figure 11-15. *GitHub Actions view*

If the view says that GitHub Actions have not yet been enabled, then simply follow the on-screen instructions (which will take you directly to the configuration) to enable "All Actions" on your repository.

From here, you can now select "Run workflow" and then select the branch you want to manually run the workflow on, for example, "Main," as shown in Figure 11-16.

Figure 11-16. *Manually run workflow for a branch*

Assuming everything was configured correctly, and no errors occurred, a successful run should appear in the "Actions view" along with the results of that run, as in Figure 11-17.

Figure 11-17. *GitHub Actions result*

Troubleshooting

If for whatever reason the workflow did not run successfully, here are a few things to check:

- Make sure your License Activation request was pregenerated using the GitHub Actions provided by GameCI and not from your machine.

- Ensure you have used the "contents" from the **ACTIVATION FILE** (.ulf) you downloaded from Unity and not the activation request file (.alf). The contents should start with the following:

```
<?xml version="1.0" encoding="UTF-8"?><root>
    <License id="Terms">
```

- Ensure the "**PROJECTPATH**" to your project is set correctly, especially if you are using a subfolder (as in the example). If your project is in the root, make sure the path is NOT set.

- Hosted agents WILL eventually eat into your free credit, so make sure to use the "**CACHE**" action to store the Library folder at a minimum. But beware, if your dependencies radically change, this may affect your build and need clearing every once in a while, because Unity…

With the basics out of the way, let us now look to setting up self-hosting for GitHub. If you have spare hardware lying around doing nothing or do not mind using your development PC in the background, you might as well make the most use of it and save some pennies.

Running on hosted agents is perfectly fine, but you do need to keep an eye on usage and costs.

Self-Hosting Requirements with GitHub Actions

Note at the time of writing, GameCI does not work well with Windows-based self-hosted agents as most of their GitHub actions use technology specifically for Linux-based hosts. I have included instructions for getting GameCI building working on Windows later in this chapter for reference should you wish to try it; if you have experience with Linux, then the steps are the same as detailed as follows, so feel free to try it. But for running self-hosted agents successfully on Windows, we need to use a different style of workflow, which is detailed as follows.

Like with Azure Pipelines, self-hosted agents are quick and easy to set up and have very similar prerequisites, such as

- A dedicated user account that can access BOTH the PC in question and the GitHub automation.

- The operating system to support a specific build operation, Windows for Windows/Android/Web builds, Mac for iOS/Android/Web builds, etc.

- The required software to run the build, for example, Unity, required SDKs, etc.

- Permanent access to the Internet; it is a cloud operation at the end of the day, and GitHub needs to send builds to the machine.

- The required scripting support and libraries for automation, usually GIT, NodeJS, PowerShell, Bash, or a combination (which will depend on your workflow).

- Power – The machine will need to be on for the times when automation is required.

The environment should be the same as any other development machine, and there is no limit to how many you can have; in fact, if the machine is powerful enough, you can install MANY agents on the same host to improve concurrency. The choice is up to you – several machines, each with the ability to execute a single build, or a bigger machine to run many.

Configuring a GitHub Self-Hosting Agent

With GitHub, Microsoft has greatly simplified the setting up of Agents, removing the need for any additional setup or configuration within your GitHub organization or project; you can still view what is set up and manage them (force remove), but there is nothing to "configure."

To configure a new agent, we need the agent key that uniquely identifies the specific repository which can be accessed from the "New self-hosted runner" button from "Project ➤ Settings ➤ Actions ➤ Runners" (the same for an organization if you want to set up agents for all repositories). Figure 11-18 shows this.

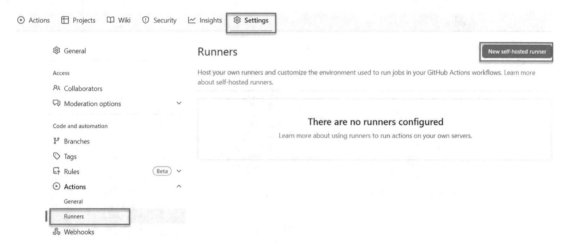

Figure 11-18. *GitHub Actions runners view*

Clicking this button will present the guide for setting up a self-hosted runner on the machine of your choice (Figure 11-19).

Runners / Create self-hosted runner

Adding a self-hosted runner requires that you download, configure, and execute the GitHub Actions Runner. By downloading and configuring the GitHub Actions Runner, you agree to the GitHub Terms of Service or GitHub Corporate Terms of Service, as applicable.

Runner image

○ macOS   ○ Linux   ◉ Windows

Architecture

x64

Download

We recommend configuring the runner under "\actions-runner". This will help avoid issues related to service identity folder permissions and long path restrictions on Windows.

```
# Create a folder under the drive root
$ mkdir actions-runner; cd actions-runner
# Download the latest runner package
$ Invoke-WebRequest -Uri
https://github.com/actions/runner/releases/download/v2.305.0/actions-runner-win-x64-
2.305.0.zip -OutFile actions-runner-win-x64-2.305.0.zip
# Optional: Validate the hash
$ if((Get-FileHash -Path actions-runner-win-x64-2.305.0.zip -Algorithm
SHA256).Hash.ToUpper() -ne
'3a4afe6d9056c7c63ecc17f4db32148e946454f2384427b0a4565b7690ef7420'.ToUpper()){ throw
'Computed checksum did not match' }
# Extract the installer
$ Add-Type -AssemblyName System.IO.Compression.FileSystem ;
[System.IO.Compression.ZipFile]::ExtractToDirectory("$PWD/actions-runner-win-x64-
2.305.0.zip", "$PWD")
```

Configure

```
# Create the runner and start the configuration experience
$ ./config.cmd --url https://github.com/SimonDarksideJ/TheMostAwesomeGameEverMade --token
AANVYEW3XNGVNIZOQ4FBCY3ESIY50
# Run it!
$ ./run.cmd
```

Using your self-hosted runner

```
# Use this YAML in your workflow file for each job
runs-on: self-hosted
```

For additional details about configuring, running, or shutting down the runner, please check out our product docs.

Figure 11-19. *Self-hosted runner setup*

The instructions are quite detailed and are intended to be run from a "Command Prompt" window, although if you prefer, you can just download the agent from the URL provided (which will update in the instructions when the version of the agent updates), extract it, and then begin.

For example, the agent URL in the screenshot provided points to

`https://github.com/actions/runner/releases/download/v2.303.0/`
`actions-runner-win-x64-2.303.0.zip`

which can be copied into a browser window to simply download it.

The flow is like this:

- Download the agent.

- Create a folder on your machine where the agents are intended to be run from, for example, "C:\G", keeping the name short.

I recommend that you have a folder for holding all agents and then subfolders for each agent you wish to run, even if it is only one. Allow for expansion in the future.

- Extract the agent zip to a subfolder in the preceding folder using the name of the intended agent, for example, "MyAgent01"; again, keep the name short but recognizable.

- Open a new ADMINISTRATIVE command prompt, especially if you want the agent to be started with the machine. This can be done by pressing "Win/Start", typing "CMD", and then selecting "Run as Administrator" (which may also prompt you for your password, depending on your setup).

If you intend to run the agent as a service in the background, you will need an Admin command prompt for it to have sufficient permissions to install the service. If you only ever want to run the agent manually, you can skip this. For Mac and Linux, this is slightly different, so check the specific "Mac Users and Build Hosts" section.

- Copy the "Configure" URL from the instructions (it is unique to each repository), and you are ready to begin.

If you are ready, you can move on to the "Configuring the Host" section; for Mac/Linux users, here's a little note.

Mac Users and Build Hosts

A small note/section for users creating Mac agents on an Apple Mac they have lying around to do iOS automation. This has caused me endless amounts of fun for the additional limitations placed on Apple developers to get their projects built.

On a Mac, the automation is the currently logged on user; there is no such thing as a background user/account (that I am aware of); even running the automation as a "service" requires the user that installed the service to be logged on for the automation agent to even start, and that user MUST remain logged on for automation to run.

Effectively, Mac build hosts are dedicated machines (unlike Windows) and can only be used for automation.

When setting up a Mac, ensure

- The automation user is logged on; if restarted, this user will need to be logged on again or set up to automatically log on.

- The automation user needs SPECIFIC access to files and folders on the host; just being an admin is not enough; you may need to check folder permissions to ensure they have read and write access to all required folders.

- You need to override the Mac default ability to block processes from automatically running on the host (see the following command) or MANUALLY allow each and every DLL required to run automation on the Mac.

- The Mac user will also need access to an Apple developer account which has access to the Apple organization. Thankfully though, this does not need to be separate and can be any valid Apple developer account.

- The Unity installation needs to be set up and registered for building Apple apps. Just run a few end-to-end tests building an app and PUBLISHING to TestFlight. This will save you HOURS of head scratching later.

I found the following command which can enable "Allow apps downloaded from Anywhere":

sudo spctl --master-disable

Source: `https://github.com/microsoft/azure-pipelines-agent/issues/2457`

I wish you well on your journey to retain your hair while getting automation running on a Mac.

Configuring the Host

With your command prompt/terminal window open in the folder of the agent (make sure you have navigated to the agent folder or it will not work), we can begin; simply paste the "**CONFIG**" command into the window, which should look as follows:

```
config.cmd --url https://GitHub.com/SimonDarksideJ/
TheMostAwesomeGameEverMade --token <your private token>
```

For Windows, ignore the "." at the beginning of the instructions; however, on Mac and Linux, you do!

What follows are a set of questions to get you up and running quite quickly:

1. First, you will be asked for a "**RUNNER GROUP**" which is only needed for Enterprise GitHub organizations; you can simply hit "Enter" here to continue.

Runner groups are a way for organizations to organize large amounts of GitHub agents according to their needs; it also allows them to specify additional permissions/access controls over specific groups. However, it is only available to GitHub Enterprise customers; for more information, check the following link:

https://docs.github.com/en/actions/hosting-your-own-runners/ managing-self-hosted-runners/managing-access-to-self-hosted-runners-using-groups

---

2. You will then be asked what to call the agent so it can be recognized in GitHub; use the folder name of the agent to keep everything aligned.

3. If you need more granular access to specific runners, you can specify custom "**TAGS**" for the runner; these are used when you specify which agent the workflow "runs on" in the YAML. The default is "self-hosted" and some additional tags that signify the operating system and architecture of the machine. Just hit enter to accept the defaults or add additional ones (without quotes) separated by a ",".

4. To finish off the agent setup, you need to enter a "work" folder where everything the agent does will be stored; again, keep the path small to reduce the path size. I always prefer to set it to simply "w".

With the agent created, you then need to decide whether you will run the agent manually or automatically, and this is where the path differs on Windows as opposed to Mac or Linux.

Windows

For Windows, you will be prompted whether you want to run the agent as a service or not; if you select "Y," it will prompt you for the administrative account you want the service to be run under and its password. This will then create a new background service for the agent which will start automatically when the Host starts. You can either accept the default (which to be honest I usually do) or select a specific account, such as the automation user account that you set up; the choice is up to you.

Mac/Linux

For Mac and Linux, the service will not be installed automatically; you have to do this manually using the "**./svc.sh**" script which is pretty automatic; however, on Mac at least (I have not personally installed it on Linux, unless you count Mac), the story does not end there, as although the service is registered, you need to enable the script to be able to run. Either you will need to go to the Apple Preferences ➤ Security window and enable each and every DLL to run (I did it once being ignorant of Mac operation; it was not fun) or run the SUDO command mentioned earlier in the agent folder to ignore security for the scripts in the agent folder. Either way, you should ask your respective Mac person to help, or do as I have done, which is again up to you.

Agent Completion

If you have typed everything in correctly, not missed any spaces, selected the right accounts, and done all the bits, you should have a command prompt result like the one in Figure 11-20.

Figure 11-20. Windows install result

Fear ye not, many slip-ups can happen while installing the agent; to restart, you will need to uninstall the current agent before starting again using the following command:

`config.cmd remove`

or on a Mac:

`./config.sh remove`

which will uninstall the agent from the host and deregister it from GitHub. You will need your "Runner Token" (which can be found in the "New Runner" instructions) to update GitHub or remove it manually from the UI. Make sure you want to, as the remove command does not ask you if you want to, it just DOES IT!

With the agent installed, you can check the GitHub Runners interface to see your new agent in all its glory up and running (hopefully), as shown in Figure 11-21.

Runners

New self-hosted runner

Host your own runners and customize the environment used to run jobs in your GitHub Actions workflows. Learn more about self-hosted runners.

Runners	Status
🖥 **myagent01** (self-hosted) (Windows) (X64)	● Offline ⋯

Figure 11-21. Runners view

You can also see the "**Tags**" you defined for the runner; if you need to change the tags, you can click the runner and click the "**cog**" icon next to the "**Labels**," which will allow you to create new tags/labels for future use.

Clicking the agent will show you what the agent is currently up to, not much at this point as we have not updated our workflow to use it (Figure 11-22).

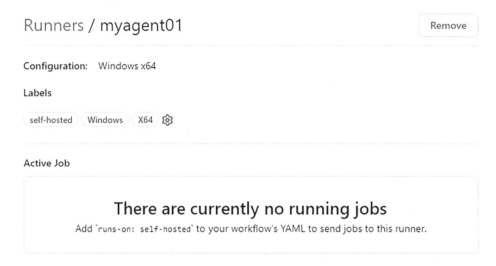

Figure 11-22. Runner status

Using Custom Scripts to Build Unity

At the time of writing, GameCI does not support running automation locally, as it is designed for hosted environments; if/when this changes, you can check the "GameCI Self-Hosted on Windows" section for more details.

The best way of building Unity on a self-hosted Windows machine is to use Unity natively through scripts; this might sound daunting but is quite easy as I have already done 99% of the work for you (especially as I use these techniques on many open source and work style projects).

I may publish the scripts as public GitHub actions, given there are not many others available and those that are are not documented or updated regularly.

Switching from using GameCI to your custom scripts requires a slightly different approach which requires the use of some custom scripting (which I have built for you) that performs the following tasks:

- Get the Unity version number from the Unity project.

- Set up access to the Unity Hub and verify it is installed (it is recommended to use the Unity Hub to manage Unity installs).

- Check the required version of Unity is installed for the project (this needs to be managed manually, because Unity...). However, the script has been updated to look for "any" version of Unity within the current release, for example, 2021.2 will check for any 2022.2 release installed.

- Prepare editor commands for use based on the install location determined by the Unity Hub.

- Prepare logging, so you have a log output from the build (essential if there are issues).

- Run the unit tests (if any are available) in the project and perform the initial compile.

- Finally, create a build for the target platform and upload it.

The script I have built does all the preceding tasks and simply asks for the following inputs which we will go through in an updated YAML:

- ***targetPlatform*** (same as GameCI) – To indicate which platform to build for.

- (Optional) ***projectPath*** (same as GameCI) – To set a subfolder if your Unity project is not in the root of your repository.

- (Optional) ***unityHubPath*** – If you installed the Unity Hub to a custom folder, the script needs to know where to find it. Do yourself a favor and always install the Hub in its default location, because Unity.... 😵

- (Optional) ***buildOnTestFail*** – If you have unit tests and still want a build to be produced if the tests fail, this will override the default behavior which will prevent creating a build if failures are found.

The script is in the example repository, but is maintained in the open source Reality Collective project for reusable GitHub Actions workflows (you can check out the others if you wish when you get more experienced) here:

```
https://github.com/realitycollective/reusableworkflows/blob/main/.
github/workflows/rununitybuild.yml
```

The script is quite long, so I will not paste it here in the book. It is best to read it online and check out the latest version.

To continue, simply download the script and place it in your **.GITHUB/WORKFLOWS** folder ready for use.

With the script in place, we need to update our build YAML accordingly, but as we are using a separate script (called a reusable workflow), we need to reorder how we lay things out. Ultimately, the script is exactly the same, we just need to apply it differently.

I have created a separate YAML file called "pipeline-selfhosted.yml" to store the new build configuration.

```yaml
name: GitHub Actions example using scripting for self-hosting

on:
  workflow_dispatch:

jobs:
  checkout:
    name: Checkout
    runs-on: self-hosted
    steps:
      - name: Starting
        run: echo 'Starting...'

      # Checkout
      - name: Checkout repository
        uses: actions/checkout@v3

  build:
    name: Build my project
    needs: checkout
    uses: SimonDarksideJ/TheMostAwesomeGameEverMade/.GitHub/workflows/
    rununitybuild.yml@main
    with:
      targetPlatform: StandaloneWindows
      projectPath: TheMostAwesomeGameEverMade

  Upload:
    name: Upload project
    needs: build
    runs-on: self-hosted
    steps:
      # Output
      - uses: actions/upload-artifact@v3
        with:
          name: Build
          path: TheMostAwesomeGameEverMade/build
```

For the astute of you, you should notice that instead of a single "Job" with multiple steps, there are now three "Jobs" each with separate tasks:

1. Job 1 – Check out the repository and clone (copy) it locally.

2. Job 2 – Build the project using the script provided. The path to the script NEEDS to also include the "GitHub account name" and the "repository name" in the path as shown earlier.

3. Job 3 – Upload the output of the build to GitHub so that it can be downloaded and run. This will only happen if the build was successful, and a build was generated.

Each Job depends on the previous Job using the "needs" property which lists the other Jobs the current job requires to be run first.

If you now run the workflow and provided you have set all the parameters correctly (especially making sure to set a ***projectPath*** if your project is in a subfolder as in the example), then you should see an output similar to the one shown in Figure 11-23 on the completion of its execution.

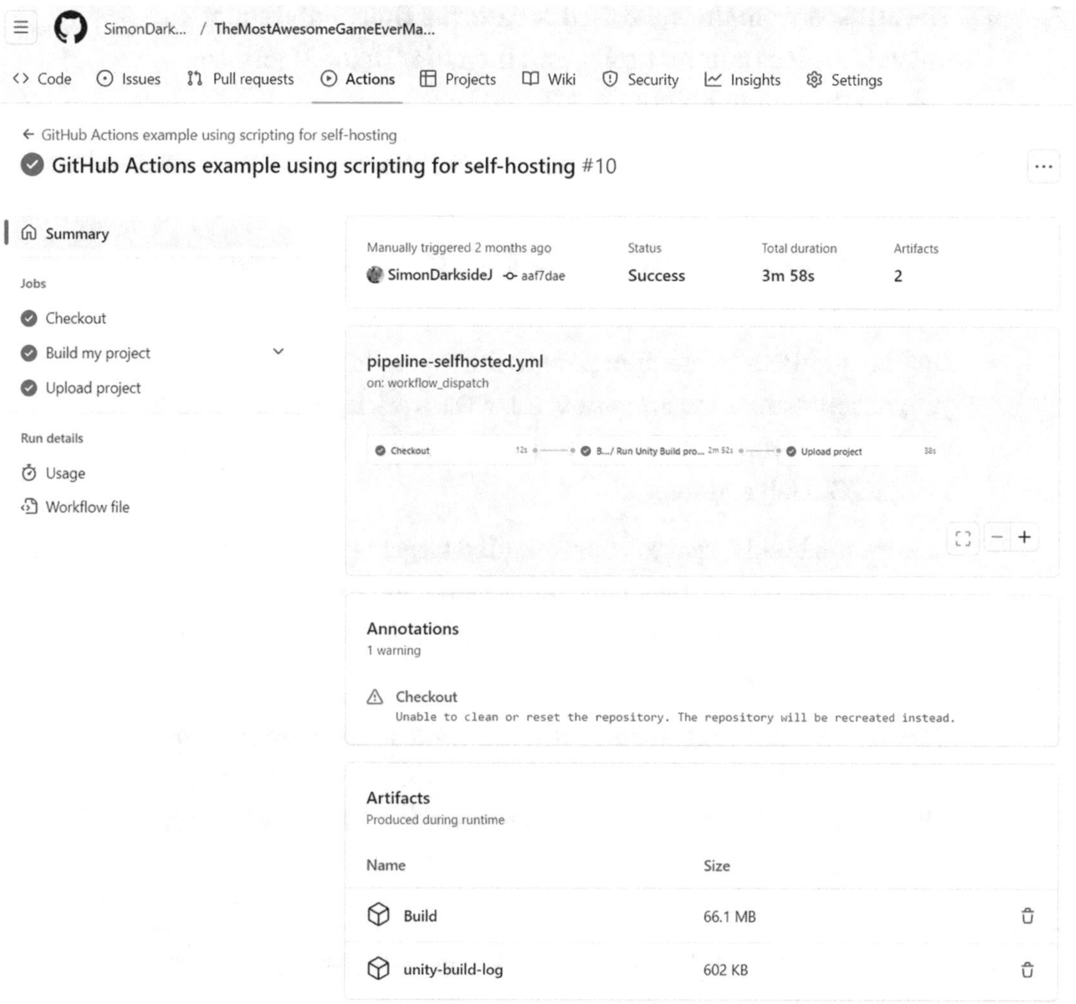

Figure 11-23. *Self-hosted script–based action*

The report shows

- The workflow execution is in a nice graphical format (you can click on each to see its output); if the output is not as shown, check your "needs" parameters for each Job.

- Any annotations or warnings from the automation run, usually reports from Actions used or messages generated from the workflow.

- The artifacts from the build, in this case, the Unity build script uploads the logs automatically, and then the "Upload" job also uploads the output build.

And now it is up and running. The only changes you need to make to customize it for your own project are

- Make sure to copy the "***rununitybuild.yml***" script into your repository.

- Update the "Uses" statement path to the preceding script to match your account and repository (it WILL NOT work if you leave it as it is now, as scripts MUST be in the same repository to work, or use PUBLIC GitHub actions).

- Change the build target to your intended target or make several copies of the "Build" Job if you want several platforms built (see below); just make sure to update the "Needs" for the Upload job to wait until all builds are done.

- Update the script trigger; currently, it is using a "***workflow_dispatch***" which means it needs to be manually run; you may want to run it whenever code is pushed to a branch or when a PR is made to the repository.

Check out the workflows for the Reality Collective packages to see various examples of triggers:

```
https://github.com/realitycollective/com.realitytoolkit.core/
tree/development/.github/workflows
```

Have fun and keep testing/building.

Example Multibuild Script

```
name: GitHub Actions example using scripting for self-hosting to build
multiple targets

# Run workflow each time code is pushed to the repository
on: [push]

jobs:
  checkout:
    name: Checkout
    runs-on: self-hosted
    steps:
      - name: Starting
        run: echo 'Starting...'

      # Checkout
      - name: Checkout repository
        uses: actions/checkout@v3

# Build the Windows Platform, only needs checkout.
  buildWindows:
    name: Build my project
    needs: checkout
    uses: SimonDarksideJ/TheMostAwesomeGameEverMade/.GitHub/workflows/
    rununitybuild.yml@main
    with:
      targetPlatform: StandaloneWindows
      projectPath: TheMostAwesomeGameEverMade

# Build the WebGL Platform, only needs checkout.
  buildWebGL:
    name: Build my project
    needs: checkout
    uses: SimonDarksideJ/TheMostAwesomeGameEverMade/.GitHub/workflows/
    rununitybuild.yml@main
    with:
      targetPlatform: WebGL
      projectPath: TheMostAwesomeGameEverMade
```

```
# Build the Android Platform, only needs checkout.
  buildAndroid:
    name: Build my project
    needs: checkout
    uses: SimonDarksideJ/TheMostAwesomeGameEverMade/.GitHub/workflows/
    rununitybuild.yml@main
    with:
      targetPlatform: Android
      projectPath: TheMostAwesomeGameEverMade

# Upload built projects to GitHub once ALL builds are complete
  Upload:
    name: Upload project
    needs: [buildWindows, buildWebGL, buildAndroid]
    runs-on: self-hosted
    steps:
      # Output
      - uses: actions/upload-artifact@v3
        with:
          name: Build
          path: TheMostAwesomeGameEverMade/build
```

The preceding script will run whenever code is pushed to the repository, then check out the code and run all three builds concurrently (provided there are enough agents to do so). Once the builds are all complete, the Build output is uploaded to GitHub.

GameCI Self-Hosted on Windows

Note at the time of writing, GameCI does not include images for building WebGL or Android on a Windows host. An issue has been logged, but for now GameCI builds on Windows are limited to Windows Standalone and Windows UWP only. Some images also do not work as described or fail to run.

Getting GameCI actions working on Windows requires a few extra hoops than your normal deployment, requiring the following:

- Windows Subsystems for Linux (WSL)

- Docker for Windows

- A little extra environment configuration

It is not that bad, and if you wish to retain the option for still using hosted GameCI builds without radically changing your pipeline, then it is possible.

To get GameCI running on Windows, follow these steps:

1. Install WSL using the following instructions:

   ```
   https://learn.microsoft.com/en-us/windows/wsl/install
   ```

   Essentially, just run "***wsl –install***" from an administrative command prompt. Although note you will need to enable Virtualization on your PC, which the guide walks you through.

2. Install Docker for Windows using the following instructions:

   ```
   https://learn.microsoft.com/en-us/windows/wsl/tutorials/
   wsl-containers
   ```

   The installer has been updated since the guide was created and WSL2 is used by default, so simply run the installer.

3. Update your "Path" to include the folder where the Linux Bash tools are located:

    Edit your environment variables (***Start ➤ Environment Variables***) and edit the Path option in the System environment variables; you will need to add an extra folder to the list to "***C:\ Program Files\Git\bin***" (installed by Git for Windows) to enable access to Linux Shell commands needed by GameCI.

Done.

Now you can update your YAML, based on the GameCI YAML template (**pipeline-gameci.yml**), to update the "runs-on" parameter with the following:

```
runs-on: self-hosted
```

or

```
runs-on: windows
```

Now instead of using the expensive Microsoft hosting for the intensive task of building and publishing our Unity project, we can use our much reasonably priced hardware situated at our desk.

Summary

With GitHub Actions, the barrier for entry is much lower, and you will find more resources and help in the community than you would for Unity Cloud Build or Azure Pipelines, mainly because it is newer but also because of how accessible it is. Although be warned, I have lost many an hour just tinkering with a pipeline as the web tools make it so easy to keep tweaking it and seeing the result, then you look up and it is 4 am!

A few additional things you can try out:

- Try out the multibuild script for multiple platforms.

- Try installing an agent on a different operating system and then updating your pipeline to run some builds on Windows and other Builds on Mac at the same time, if you can.

- Do not just have Unity build script, also maintain your repository, for example, the Reality Collective has actions scripts to make versioning, publishing of packages, and so on. Others I have seen also update release notes and documentation; keep playing.

- Have a look into AppCenter integration and deploying your builds through AppCenter automatically.

We have completed the outlined scope of the services available, and it is now up to you to choose which path you follow, but remember there is no one fixed rule or guide that you can only use one of these paths; many studios, including myself, use multiple services based on what they are good at. For example, I use GitHub actions for all my testing, repository management, and project management, but I use Azure Pipelines to generate the builds themselves (its integration with deployment services is slightly better). Repositories can contain build configurations for multiple services, and hosts can also install agents from the services you need to use, so you do not need separate equipment.

In the end, only implement what makes sense to you or your business, start small, do the little things that take up most of your time, and then work toward the bigger tasks. At the end of the day, if you are spending too much time managing your automation rather than building your game or project, then you are not saving time; maintain a balanced approach. That being said, it was a huge relief the week I spend working on the automation scripts to simply manage the versioning and packaging of the release pipeline for the Reality Collective, as it has saved countless hours and removed the possibility of human error.

CHAPTER 12

Final Notes

Woah, what a road it has been that we have traveled along, and while our journey has come to an end, I hope yours has only just begun. The world of automation is wondrous, and its possibilities are almost endless, so long as you keep your wits about you. Frodo did not blindly wander off without a plan to do what was needed, oh wait, bad example 🦶.

In recap, we have

- Got to know the ins and outs of automation, language, terminology, and form.

- Delved into time-saving techniques to do all the cross-checks, validations, and grammar.

- Marveled at the idea of testing, especially unit testing. Gazed in horror and the effort required but settled by how much of your skin it can save in the long run.

- Rummaged around in the depths of Unity to understand what goes into making a build, not as easy as just hitting "build and run," but safer and more secure.

- And finally, peered behind the curtain of the three major operators in the space for building Unity projects. It is not all, but that would make for a much longer title.

My aim was to show you the road, understand how to make steps, and build a common understanding across the fields of automation, seeing the commonalities and learning to read the automation language, no matter which vendor country you venture into, as they all share a common root and structure (well, except for UGS, but not everyone is perfect).

© Simon Jackson 2023
S. Jackson, *Accelerating Unity Through Automation*, https://doi.org/10.1007/978-1-4842-9508-3_12

Ultimately, with a grasp of what is out there, you can plan for which tools and which vendor to use based upon the circumstances of your project, for instance:

- If it is tiny, maybe just use Unity, who needs this automation anyway.

- If you are a little more pragmatic, have a template of automation that you use for every project, no matter the size.

- Want it quick and easy without thinking about it, throw it into Unity's DevOps system. A few clicks and off it builds (just watch the bank account).

- Understand when to go from a single project to using UPM packages to split up your Unity project, and know how to build and automate everything both at the micro and macroscopic levels.

- Never be afraid to experiment, just throw up a repo, hook it up to your dev machine as a self-hosted agent, and play with anything.

You will still likely have questions, which is completely natural in this area, like machine learning, AI, and cloud services; there is so much to learn. However, with automation, there is no wrong answer, and in many occasions, it might take a fair bit of trial and error to get the outcomes you want, but knowing what is possible is the first step in achieving your goals.

So onward weary traveler, you will likely see me out there in the vast interwebs, and feel free to chat as I have always got an ear and I am usually willing to help, if the sun is facing east and a steady cross-wind is blowing.

Have fun.

Index

A

Printed in the United States
by Baker & Taylor Publisher Services